A Christian Is . . .

by

Mike Willis

truth
BOOKS

ISBN 10: 1-58427-367-4

ISBN 13: 978-1-58427-3677

truth
BOOKS

Guardian of Truth Foundation
CEI Bookstore
220 S. Marion St., Athens, AL 35611
truthbooks.net
1-855-49-BOOKS or 1-855-492-6657

Table of Contents

Dedication

A man is truly blessed to have a son. How much more richly blessed he is to have a son who walks in the pathway of righteousness. In appreciation for the moral purity he demonstrated through his teenage years, his excellent song leading, and his active participation in the work of the local church, this book is affectionately dedicated to my only son:

Corey Michael Willis

A Christian Is . . . A Child of God

In this series of lessons, we propose to understand what a Christian is by looking at the terms by which he is called. The Christian is known as a "child of God" (1 Jn. 3:9-10). When God called us out of darkness and into his marvelous light, he promised to be a Father to us and we would be sons and daughters to him.

> Wherefore come out from among them, and be ye separate, said the Lord, and touch not the unclean thing; and I will receive you, and will be a Father unto you, and ye shall be my sons and daughters, saith the Lord Almighty (2 Cor. 6:17-18).

The promise of sustaining a Father-child relationship to God should motivate us to leave the world and turn to God.

Two Spiritual Families

There are but two spiritual families. One is either a child of God or a child of the Devil. John wrote, "Whosoever is born of God doth not commit sin; for his seed remaineth in him: and he cannot sin, because he is born of God. In this the children of God are manifest, and the children of the devil: whosoever doeth not righteousness is not of God, neither he that loveth not his brother" (1 Jn. 3:9-10). Jesus contrasted those who were children of God and children of the Devil as well (Jn. 8:42-44). Mankind is divided into two categories: children of God and children of the Devil. Those who are children of God are Christians; if a person is not a Christian, he is a child of the Devil.

Only Christians have the privilege of addressing God as their Father (Matt. 6:9). Children of the devil have no more right to address God as Father than one who is not a member of my family has of addressing me as "father." Hence, the privilege of prayer is a privilege to children of God.

Child: A Relationship With God

John said, "Behold, what manner of love the Father hath bestowed upon us, that we should be called the sons of God" (1 Jn. 3:1). When one considers all of the possible relationships that one could sustain to God, he should marvel that God has so richly blessed us in allowing us to sustain the intimate relationship of Father-child to him. Here are some relationships he could have sustained to us: (a) Enemies because we have sinned against his will; (b) Deistic relationship – that of an uncaring God who has wound up the world and removed himself from it, waiting for it to wind down; a detached relationship; (c) Playthings – we could be the "mouse in the maze" to God; etc.

We became God's children through the new birth when we were "born of God" (Jn. 1:13; 3:3-5). His seed abides in us since we are born of God (1 Jn. 3:9). The seed that brings conception is the word of God (1 Pet. 1:23f; 1 Cor. 4:15). Paul wrote, "For ye are all the children of God by faith in Christ Jesus. For as many of you as have been baptized into Christ have put on Christ" (Gal. 3:26-27). We have received the "adoption of sins" (Gal. 4:5). A person becomes a child of God through hearing the gospel preached, believing it with all of his heart, repenting of his sins, confessing his faith in Jesus, and being baptized for the remission of his sins (Rom. 10:10,17; Mk. 16:15-16; Lk. 13:3; Matt. 10:32; Acts 8:37; 2:38; 22:16). This is the only way one can become a child of God. There are no children born of God in any other way. A person can know that he is a child of God when the testimony of his spirit agrees with the testimony of the Holy Spirit (Rom. 8:16). For example, the Holy Spirit told me to believe in Jesus, my spirit testifies that I have believed in Jesus; the Holy Spirit testifies that I must repent of my sins, my spirit testifies that I have repented of my sins, etc.

There are some important blessings that come from being a child of God.

1. God is his Father. Paul wrote, "And because ye are sons, God hath sent forth the Spirit of his Son into your hearts, crying, Abba, Father" (Gal. 4:6). "For ye have not received the spirit of bondage again to fear; but ye have received the Spirit of adoption, whereby we cry, Abba, Father" (Rom. 8:15). The emphasis of these verses is our attitude toward God; we do not approach him as a slave does his master but as a son does his father. "Abba" is "an Aramaic word. . . . It approximates to a personal name, in contrast to 'Father,' with which it is always joined in the N.T. . . . 'Abba' is the word framed by the lips of infants, and betokens unreasoning trust; 'father' expresses an intelligent apprehension of the relationship. The two together express the love and intelligent confidence of the child" (W.E. Vine, *An Expository Dictionary of New Testament Words*, Vol. I, p. 9). Our relationship to God is compared to a father/son relationship. We do not have a spirit of fear or the spirit of a slave when we approach God.

2. His concern over our prayers. Because of our relationship to God, we can approach him in prayer as "Our Father which art in heaven" (Matt. 6:9). Because of this relationship, we know that God listens to and answers our prayers. Jesus said, "Ask, and it shall be given you; seek, and ye shall find; knock, and it shall be opened unto you: for every one that asketh receiveth; and he that seeketh findeth; and to him that knocketh it shall be opened. Or what man is there of you, whom if his son ask bread, will he give him a stone? Or if he ask a fish, will he give him a serpent? If ye then, being evil, know how to give good gifts unto your children, how much more shall your Father which is in heaven give good things to them that ask him?" (Matt. 7:7-11).

John wrote, "And this is the confidence that we have in him, that, if we ask any thing according to his will, he heareth us: and if we know that he hears us, whatsoever we ask, we know that we have the petitions that we desired of him" (1 Jn. 5:14-15). The poet said, "What a privilege to carry, Everything to God in prayer" (Joseph Scriven, "What A Friend We Have In Jesus").

3. The right of inheritance. As children of God, we are also heirs of God. Paul wrote, "The Spirit itself beareth witness with our spirit, that we are the children of God: and if children, then heirs; heirs of God, and joint-heirs with Christ" (Rom. 8:16-17). We look forward to receiving an inheritance that is "incorruptible, and undefiled, and that fadeth not away, reserved in heaven for you, who are kept by the power of God through faith" (1 Pet. 1:4-5). We shall dwell in the mansions which Jesus has prepared for us (Jn. 14:1-3), in the city of God so beautifully described in Revelation 21.

4. The obligation to become like God. Because we are children of God, we should become like God. "Be ye therefore followers of God, as dear children" (Eph. 5:1). I can remember helping my Daddy plant a garden when I was a child. We always borrowed my Uncle Jim's one-eyed mule to plow our garden. I used to walk behind my Daddy as he plowed, trying to step in his tracks. In the same way, we should follow in the steps of God. Just as my father was a log hauler, as a child I wanted to be a long hauler. Similarly, we who are children of God ought to imitate our Father. We walk in the light as he is in the light (1 Jn. 1:7), as he is holy we should be holy (1 Pet. 1:15-16), and as God is love we should love one another (1 Jn. 4:7-8).

Brethren: A Relationship With One Another

Whereas the word "child" refers to our relationship with God, "brother" refers to our relationship other children of God. Every person who is born of God is my brother; where God has a child, I have a brother. Those who obey the Father are children of God and my brothers and sisters (Matt. 12:46-50). Those who disobey the Father are not brethren.

1. Brethren assist each other. (a) Brethren are to provide emotional support to one another. There should exist among brethren "the same care one for another. And whether one member suffer, all the members suffer with it; or one member be honoured, all the members rejoice with it" (1 Cor. 12:25-26). (b) Brethren should provide physical support to one another (1 Jn. 3:17). When a brother has need for food, clothing, and shelter, his brethren should supply that need. (c) Brethren should provide spiritual support for one another. When a brother is overtaken in a trespass, his brethren should work to restore him (Gal. 6:1).

2. Brethren should get along with one another. Abraham spoke to Lot, "Let there be no strife, I pray thee, between me and thee, and between my herdmen and thy herdmen; *for we be brethren*" (Gen. 13:8). The local church should have that same attitude toward strife among brethren. Brethren who bite and devour one another destroy each other spiritually (Gal. 5:15). Sometimes brethren refer to each other as "brother" but treat each other as enemies by gossip, slander, and other maliciousness.

Practicing hospitality toward one another (1 Pet. 4:9) is one way of cultivating warm feelings toward each other. Putting the other's well being above our own (Phil. 2:4) contributes to amicable relationships between brethren. Rude, self-willed, domineering, factious brethren will destroy brotherly love in a congregation.

Conclusion

What is a Christian? He is a child of God, a son of the King! He is striving to become like his Father. He is a brother to every other child of God. Those who are not children of God are not Christians. Those who do not treat other Christians as their brethren forfeit their right to be children of God; they are "cursed children" (2 Pet. 2:14).

Questions

1. What promise did God make to those who forsake wickedness to serve him (2 Cor. 6:17-18)? _____

    _____

2. What two spiritual families exist (1 Jn. 3:9-10)? _____

    _____

3. How does one become a part of the family of God? _____

    _____

4. How does one know that he is a child of God (Rom. 8:16). Explain your answer. _____

    _____

5. How many children does God have who have not done this? _____
6. Why is being a child of God a privilege (1 Jn. 3:1)? _____

    _____

7. What is the spirit of sonship (in contrast to the spirit of bondage) in Galatians 4:6 and Romans 8:15? _____

_____

8. What privilege in prayer does a child of God have that is not available to those who are not Christians (Matt. 6:9; 7:7-11; 1 Jn. 5:14-15)? _____

9. What inheritance is given to the child of God (Rom. 8:16-17)? _____

_____

_____

10. How does being a child of God obligate us (Eph. 5:1)? _____

_____

11. According to Matthew 12:46-50, who are Jesus' brothers and sisters? ___

_____

12. What obligation do brethren have to each other with reference to emotional support (1 Cor. 12:25-26)? _____

_____

13. How much knowledge of each other's needs must one have to be able to fulfill that obligation? _____

_____

14. What obligation do brethren have toward each other's physical needs (1 Jn. 3:17)? _____

_____

15. What does Genesis 13:8 reveal about brethren's obligation to get along with each other? _____

_____

16. What role does hospitality play in fulfilling our obligations to each other (1 Pet. 4:9)? _____

_____

17. How do poor brotherly relationships contribute to division?_____

_____

_____

True or False
____ 1. A person can become a child of God through faith alone.
____ 2. Those who are in denominationalism are our brothers and sisters in Christ.
____ 3. A person who rejects Jesus' teaching regarding worship (e.g., he may use instrumental music in worship) is our brother and should be received into the fellowship of the saints.
____ 4. Prayer is only a privilege for children of God.
____ 5. A person can be saved without being a child of God.

A Christian Is . . . A Believer

One of the most common titles ascribed to Christians is "believers" (cf. Acts 2:44; 4:32; 5:14). The word "believer" is translated from the Greek word *pisteuo* which is defined as follows: "to believe, also to be persuaded of, and hence, to place confidence in, to trust, signifies, in this sense of the word, reliance upon, not mere credence" (W.E. Vine, *An Expository Dictionary of New Testament Words*, Vol. I, p. 116). The object in which one believes is not inherent in the word; it must be determined from the context. Some were said to be believers in Moses (Jn. 5:46), the Scriptures (Jn. 2:22), Jesus (Jn. 3:36), and the gospel (Mk. 1:15). The word *pisteuo* and its cognates occur so many times in the New Testament that one can by no means cover all of these uses in one lesson.

The Basis of Faith: The Word of God

Paul asserted the connection between faith which leads to salvation and the revealed word of God in the following passage:

> For with the heart man believeth unto righteousness; and with the mouth confession is made unto salvation. For the Scripture said, Whosoever believeth on him shall not be ashamed. For there is no difference between the Jew and the Greek: for the same Lord over all is rich unto all that call upon him. For whosoever shall call upon the name of the Lord shall be saved. How then shall they call on him in whom they have believed? And how shall they believe in him of whom they have not heard? And how shall they hear without a preacher? And how shall they preach except they be sent? As it is written, How beautiful are the feet of them that preach the gospel of peace, and bring glad tidings of good things! But they have not all obeyed the gospel. For Esaias saith, Lord, who hath believed our report? So then faith cometh by hearing, and hearing by the word of God (Rom. 10:10-17).

From this text, we can see that faith in derived from the word of God. This is confirmed by these facts: (a) The gospel records the miracles of Jesus, giving eyewitness testimony, to enable men to believe in him to the salvation of the soul (Jn. 20:30-31). (b) A person cannot come to God without hearing and learning of him (Jn. 6:44-45). (c) Every case of New Testament conversion was preceded by preaching the word (cf. Acts 2, 8, 9, 10, 16, etc.). (d) Acts 14:2 states that Paul "so spake that a great multitude believed." (e) Peter said that the Gentiles heard the word of the gospel from his mouth and believed (Acts 15:7). Many other Scriptures, too numerous to mention, confirm that saving faith is that which is grounded in the revealed word of God.

Faith is not a "leap in the dark," as some infidel theologians assert. Denying that the existence of God and the deity of Jesus can be proved conclusively, they believe that true "faith" is the leap beyond what the available evidence actually warrants. Such is not Bible faith, nor is it noble. To believe what cannot be sustained by evidence is irrational. If one shows faith by believing what cannot be proved, he shows the greatest faith who believes what is most irrational. Furthermore, if faith is a "leap in the dark," what makes the "leap in the dark" of the Christian any different from the "leap in the dark" of the atheist, agnostic, Jew, Muslim, Hindu, or Buddhist? The infidel's concept of faith undermines the faith of Jesus Christ.

Such a view of faith reduces faith to the act of believing. There is no saving virtue in the act of the believing; the saving virtue of faith is its object – what is believed. Compare this to eating. One does not sustain life by eating, but by what he eats. If a man eats poison, he will die. He must eat wholesome food to sustain his life. Similarly, one must believe the truth to be saved from sin (Jn. 8:32). The act of believing alone will not save; one must believe the gospel to be saved.

Jesus asserted that one must accept as factual a revealed body of truth before he can be saved. He said, "If ye continue in my word, then are ye my disciples indeed; and ye shall know the truth, and the truth shall make you free" (Jn. 8:31-32). Salvation from sin is contingent upon these things: (a) There being a body of revealed truth; (b) Man's being able to comprehend that truth; (c) Man's comprehension and belief of that truth. Salvation from sin is conditioned upon belief of certain propositions of truth.

Saving faith rests firmly and squarely upon the revealed word of God. One is exercising faith when he is walking in the light of God's word. When he is not in the light of God's word, he is in darkness, regardless of his motives and intentions.

The Objects of Faith

Here are some of the propositions which one must believe to be a "believer," a Christian.

1. A Christian is a man who believes in God. Jesus said, "Let not your heart be troubled: ye believe in God, believe also in me" (Jn. 14:1). A Christian, therefore, is a person who believes in God. The author of Hebrews wrote,

"But without faith it is impossible to please him: for he that cometh to God must believe that he is, and that he is a rewarder of them that diligently seek him" (Heb. 11:6). An atheist and an agnostic do not believe that "he is, and that he is a rewarder of them that diligently seek him." To believe in God is to believe in one God, Jehovah the God of the Bible. To believe in God is to reject polytheism and idolatry. A man is not a New Testament believer who believes that there are many gods and lords. The believer rejects the gods of Hinduism, Islam, and any other humanly devised religion.

2. A Christian is a man who believes in Jesus. Jesus said, "Ye believe in God, believe also in me" (Jn. 14:1). He also said, "I said therefore unto you, that ye shall die in your sins: for if ye believe not that I am he, ye shall die in your sins" (Jn. 8:24). A New Testament believer believes what the Bible says about Jesus. He believes in the virgin birth, the miracles which Jesus performed, his atonement on Calvary, his bodily resurrection, his ascension into heaven, etc. The man who does not believe these things will be damned. The Great Commission records, "Go ye into all the world, and preach the gospel to every creature. He that believeth and is baptized shall be saved; but he that believeth not shall be damned" (Mk. 16:16). The man who rejects the gospel, the divinely revealed message of salvation through Jesus Christ, shall be damned.

There are many who call themselves Christians who are not believers. The seminaries of the mainline Protestant denominations are filled with professors and students who reject what the Bible teaches about the Christ. They deny the virgin birth, miracles, resurrection, and atonement but still claim to be Christians. If Christians are believers then these men are not Christians because they are not believers in the New Testament use of the term!

Jesus also said, "I am the way, the truth, and the life: no man cometh unto the Father, but by me" (Jn. 14:6). A believer is one who recognizes Jesus as the *only* way to salvation. Jesus is not *a* way, *a* truth, and *a* life; he is the one and only way, truth, and life. Believers in Christ recognize but one way for men to be saved from sin. Modernists who pose as Christians, as believers, reject Jesus as the only way to salvation. They should not hide their infidelity under the cloak of Christianity.

3. A Christian is a man who believes the gospel. The gospel refers to a body of revelation given to man by inspiration of Jesus Christ. It is the "faith" once for all delivered to the saints (Jude 3). The inspired revelation presents a body of doctrine to be believed by man. Christians believe this revelation and, therefore, are known as believers.

Paul described two false teachers who "made shipwreck" their faith (1 Tim. 1:19-20). These men were to be "delivered unto Satan, that they may learn not to blaspheme." What were they teaching that brought such strong condemnation? In a later epistle, Paul spoke of these men saying, ". . . who concerning the truth have erred, saying that the resurrection is past already; and overthrow the faith of some" (2 Tim. 2:17-18). These false teachers denied part of the revelation, the future resurrection of the body. Doing this made their own faith shipwreck and overthrew the faith of every man who followed them in their false doctrine.

Those who reject the teaching of God's word are not believers. There are many who profess to be Christians who reject what the Bible teaches about the role of women, homosexuality, divorce and remarriage, modest apparel, lasciviousness (for example, dancing), etc. Christians are "believers," men and women who accept what God has revealed and strive to obey him in all things, not merely those things which they chose to believe.

The Action of Faith

Faith moves man to action. A dead faith is useless and worthless. Here are some things that faith does:

1. Trust. Faith not only involves mental assent to a certain body of facts, it also means "to place confidence in, to trust." That the cognates of *pisteuo, pistis* and *pistos*, convey the ideas of "trust," "trusty, faithful, trustworthy" is not to be overlooked. This shows another aspect of faith that sometimes is overlooked. Most of us quickly admit that mental assent will not suffice to please God and would cite the example of the devils "believing and trembling" (Jas. 2:19) and the example of the Jews who believed in Jesus but did not confess him (Jn. 12:42-43) to prove it. Yet, in our zeal to add that one must obey Jesus (a perfectly legitimate activity of faith), we may have neglected the idea of *trust* which resides in the word "believe."

The one who truly believes in God and Christ is one who repudiates every method, aside from Christ, that claims to be able to save him and appeals to Jesus for salvation. The believer is truly relying upon Jesus for salvation. Paul said, "For the which cause I also suffer these things: nevertheless I am not ashamed: for I know whom I have believed, and am persuaded that he is able to keep that which I have committed unto him against that day" (2 Tim. 1:12). The salvation rests, therefore, upon Jesus' willingness and ability to forgive and not upon man's ability to obey perfectly. The man who believes in Jesus is one who has repudiated his ability to save himself and trusts in Jesus for salvation. (In this connection, notice that baptism is said to be an appeal to God for a good conscience [1 Pet. 3:21].) The man who truly trusts in Jesus should not have anxiety. The things about which most men are anxious are cares that he casts upon the Lord and "the peace of God, which passeth all understanding, shall keep your hearts and minds through Christ Jesus" (Phil. 4:6-7). The Christian is a believer who trusts in Jesus.

Trust in Jesus manifests inself in submission to the will of God. The Christian repudiates what modern psychology teaches about child rearing trusting that God knows what is best for children; the Christian rejects the modern quest for happiness in materialism, sensuality, etc., trusting that God knows what best produces man's happiness. The wise man admonished, "Trust in the Lord with all thine heart; and lean not unto thine own understanding. In all thy ways acknowledge him, and he shall direct thy paths" (Prov. 3:5-6).

2. Obedience. Obedience is as closely tied to faith as is trust. Since the sinner is utterly relying upon Jesus for salvation (and not upon his own perfect obedience or superior intelligence), he submits to the instructions of Jesus Christ. This is the "obedience of faith" (Rom. 1:5; 16:26). The true faith is the faith that takes God at his word and does what he says! That involves obedience. Where man does not take God at his word and obey him, he is not exercising faith. Because of this aspect of faith, the noun "faith" or the verb "believe" can be used to refer to the sum total of man's commitment to Jesus. Thus, one can be said to be saved by "faith," not meaning "faith only," but a "faith" that takes God at his word and does what he says.

Conclusion

To be a believer implies that one has studied the revelation of God and has reached the conclusion that the facts asserted therein are true. Accepting them to be true, the believer gives up every other foundation for acceptance before God and trusts altogether in Jesus for salvation. Trusting in Jesus, the sinner obeys him in order to be saved. As an expression of his faith, he repents of his sin and is baptized for the forgiveness of them. All who have done this can properly be described as "believers."

Questions

1. What is the meaning of "believe"? _____
    _____
    _____

2. What does describing a Christian as a "believer" denote?_____
    _____

3. How does one become a believer in Christ (Rom. 10:10-17)? _____
    _____

4. What evidences lead one to believe that faith must be grounded in the word of God? _____
    _____

5. Why is it improper to describe Bible faith as a "blind leap in the dark"?
    _____
    _____

6. What must occur in order for a person to come to God, according to John

6:44-45? _____
_____

7. What does John 8:32 reveal about truth? _____
_____

8. What must a person believe about God the Father in order to be a Christian? _____
_____

9. What must a person believe about Jesus in order to be a Christian? ____
_____

10. What does 1 Timothy 1:19-20 and 2 Timothy 2:17-18 reveal about be-
    lieving God's word? _____
_____

11. In what manner does one with "faith" in Jesus "trust" in him for salva-
    tion? _____
_____

12. In what manner must one trust in God's revelation on any matter? _____
_____

13. How is obedience related to faith (Rom. 1:5; 16:26)? _____
_____

14. What is the condition of faith which does produce obedience (Jas. 2:14-
    26)? _____
_____

15. Can one be a believer, a Christian, while rejecting anything which God has
    revealed in the Bible? Justify your answer by the Scriptures. _____
_____

Are These Christians?
1. The denominational seminary professor teaches that Jesus was the il-
   legitimate son of Mary and Joseph. Is he a Christian? _____
2. The priest of a local denomination has recently been advocating "gay
   rights" and calling for the ordination of homosexuals as priests. Is he a
   Christian? _____
3. The Pentecostal preacher is a woman. Is she a Christian? _____
4. The local Catholic priest calls himself "father" (cf. Matt. 23:9). Is he a
   Christian? _____
5. The World Council of Churches has called a moratorium on evangelizing
   those in non-Christian religions because this implies that non-Christian
   religions are inferior to the Christian religion. Is this organization made
   up of Christians? _____

If A Christian Is A Believer, What Does He Believe. . .
1. About the worship of other gods? _____
_____

2. About salvation without believing in Jesus? _____
    _____

3. About the conditions for salvation? _____
    _____

4. About the resurrection of the body? _____
    _____

5. About the role of women? _____
    _____

6. The organization of the church? _____
    _____

Matching

____ 1. Romans 10:17   a. One can know the truth
____ 2. John 20:30-31   b. One must believe in God
____ 3. John 8:32   c. The unbeliever will be damned
____ 4. Hebrews 11:6   d. Testimony produces faith
____ 5. Mark 16:15-16   e. One must trust in God's word instead of
                                     his own understanding
____ 6. Provers 3:5-6   f. Faith comes by hearing

A Christian Is . . . A Disciple

One of the most frequently used terms to designate Christians is the word "disciple" (cf. Acts 6:1, 2, 7; 9:1, 10, 25; etc.). Luke records, "And the *disciples* were called *Christians* first in Antioch" (Acts 11:26). The word "disciple" describes a Christian. A "disciple" is not something that one becomes sometime after becoming a Christian. Every man who is a Christian is a disciple. The Great Commission says, "Go therefore and *make disciples* of all nations, baptizing them (i.e, those who desire to be disciples) in the name of the Father and the Son and the Holy Spirit" (Matt. 28:19, NASB). The participle "baptizing" explains how one makes a man a disciple. Hence, a disciple is a Christian, not some special category of Christians.

The word "disciple" was a very popular term to refer to Christians in the early days of the Restoration Movement in America. Christians were known as "Disciples of Christ." So prominent did the name become that the most liberal branch of the Christian Church designates itself the "Disciples of Christ."

What is the Bible saying about a Christian when it designates him a "disciple"?

Defining the Term

The word "disciple" is translated from the Greek word *mathetes* which appears 269 times in the New Testament and is always translated "disciple." Here are several definitions of the word:

> Lit., a learner (from *manthano*, to learn, from a root *math–*, indicating thought accompanied by endeavor), in contrast to *didaskalos*, a teacher; hence it denotes one who follows one's teaching. . . . all who manifest that they are His disciples by abiding in His word (W.E. Vine, *An Expository Dictionary of New Testament Words*, Vol. I, p. 316).

> A learner, pupil, disciple: univ. opp. to *didaskalos*. . . . one who follows one's teaching (Joseph H. Thayer, *A Greek-English Lexicon of the New Testament*, p. 386).

> (1). . . The word is found in the Bible only in the Gospels and Acts. But it is good Greek, in use from Herodotus down, and always means the pupil of someone,

in contrast to the master or teacher. . . . In all cases it implies that the person not only accepts the views of the teacher, but that he is also in practice an adherent. . . (2) . . . The disciple of Christ today may be described in the words of Farrar, as "one who believes His doctrines, rests upon His sacrifice, imbibes His spirit, and imitates His example" (*International Standard Bible Encyclopedia*, Vol. II, p. 851).

The word "disciple" emphasizes the teacher-pupil relationship. It is used in the New Testament to refer to disciples of John the Baptist (Matt. 9:14), the Pharisees (Matt. 22:16), Moses (Jn. 9:28), as well as of Jesus (Matt. 12:1). In reference to the disciples of Jesus, sometimes the word is used to refer exclusively to the Twelve Apostles. (All apostles were disciples but not all disciples were apostles.)

As we examine the definition of the word "disciple," we discover several marks of a Christian emphasized by this word.

Disciples Are Learners

1. Disciples accept the role of learners from their Master, Jesus Christ. The disciple recognizes that he has a Master or Teacher (cf. Jn. 9:2; 11:8). He recognizes the position of authority which this teacher holds (Matt. 28:18). In McClintock and Strong's *Cyclopedia of Biblical, Theological, and Ecclesiastical Literature* (Vol. II, p. 815), this aspect of being a disciple is emphasized.

There are three senses in which men are sometimes called "disciples" of any other person: (1) *Incorrectly*, from their simply maintaining something that he maintains, without any profession or proof of its being derived from him . . . . (2) When certain persons *avow* that they have *adopted* the views of another, not, however, on his authority, but from holding them to be agreeable to reason or to Scripture. . . (3) When, like the disciples of Jesus, and, as it is said, of the Pythagoreans, and the adherents of certain churches, they profess to receive their system *on the authority* of their master or Church, to acquiesce in an "ipse-dixit," or to receive all that the Church receives. These three senses should be carefully kept distinct.

The last usage is that used of the disciple of Christ. The disciple of Christ recognizes Jesus' authority and submits to it. (The authority over the Christian is not the church, but Jesus.) Christians know no other Master. They submit their will to no one other than Christ. Teachers or preachers do not occupy the position that Christ holds; their teaching holds authority only insofar as it can be shown to be that of Christ.

The disciple of Jesus recognizes the limitations in his own ability to know. From human reasoning, he could not know God. He could not know if there is a God, how many gods exist, whether they are good or bad, etc. Like Jeremiah, he confesses, "O Lord, I know that the way of man is not in himself: it is not in man that walketh to direct his steps" (10:23). He follows the admonition of the Proverbs: "Trust in the Lord with all thine heart; and lean not unto thine own understanding. In all thy ways acknowledge him, and he shall direct thy paths" (3:5-6). The disciple of Christ sees in Jesus one who knows what man cannot know without divine revelation. He can reveal the Father to us because he has seen the Father (Jn. 14:9; 12:45). He can speak authoritatively about God because he is deity and was with the Father from the beginning (Jn. 1:1). Consequently, a disciple of Christ recognizes the authority of Jesus and voluntarily submits to Jesus' teaching.

If I follow Christ's teaching only when I am able logically to verify it and reject it at points with which I do not agree with, I am not a disciple. Some who claim to be "disciples" accept Jesus' authority only when it agrees with their own desires. When their will conflicts with Jesus' expressed will, they follow their will, not the teachings of Jesus. Such men are not disciples of Christ. The man who rejects what Jesus said on divorce and remarriage, worship, the church, etc. has actually made his own stubborn will his master and not the Lord Jesus Christ. He and Jesus just happen to agree on some subjects. He is not a disciple of Christ.

2. Disciples are actively involved in learning God's will. Not only do disciples recognize the authority of Jesus, they "give all diligence" to grow in the knowledge of God (2 Pet. 1:5). They understand that one can only come to Christ through the knowledge of the truth (Jn. 8:32). The disciple is drawn to God through this process: taught – learn – come (Jn. 6:44-45). No man can come to Christ until he has learned of him (cf. Rom. 10:9-17). Hearing the gospel and obeying it are necessary for one to become a disciple (Matt. 28:18-20, see NASB).

After becoming a Christian, a disciple continues to grow in the grace and knowledge of Jesus Christ (2 Pet. 3:18). After becoming a disciple, he wants to learn "all things" that Jesus has commanded him (Matt. 28:18-20). As a newborn babe, he hungers for the milk of the word in order that he may grow spiritually (2 Pet. 2:1-2). He gives heed to reading the Scriptures (1 Tim. 4:13). He recognizes his need to grow in order that he might not be tossed to and fro by false doctrine (Eph. 4:14). He realizes that over a period of time he should grow in the knowledge of Christ to the point that he can teach others (Heb. 5:11-14). Hence, he has a love for the truth that manifests itself in the habit of studying the word of God. A Christian is a person committed to the study of God's word. He is a disciple.

When Christians quit learning God's word, they cease being his disciples. Those who profess to be Christians but who never take time to read and study the word of God, never attend Bible classes, never pay attention to the sermons, etc. have ceased recognizing Jesus as a Master instructing them in how to conduct their lives and, therefore, have ceased being disciples.

3. Disciples are followers of Christ. Disciples follow in the footsteps of their Master. Paul said, "Be ye followers of me, even as I also am of Christ" (1 Cor. 11:1). Peter wrote, "For even hereunto were ye called: because Christ also suffered for us, leaving us an example, that ye should follow his steps: who did no sin, neither was guile found in his mouth" (1 Pet. 2:21-22).

To be a disciple of Christ, a person must be a follower of Jesus. "Then said Jesus unto his disciples, If any man will come after me, let him deny himself, and take up his cross, and follow me" (Matt. 16:24). Again, Jesus said, "If any man serve me, let him follow me; and where I am, there shall also my servants be: if any man serve me, him will my Father honour" (Jn. 12:26). Even as the sheep follow the shepherd, so also do Christ's sheep follow him (Jn. 10:4). The redeemed are described as "they which follow the Lamb whithersoever he goeth" (Rev. 14:4).

Whenever one has a question regarding whether or not something is right, he should ask himself, "What would Jesus do?" If Jesus would not do the questionable practice, neither should the one who claims to be a follower of Christ. Would Jesus curse or tell filthy stories? Would Jesus engage in heavy petting or go dancing? Would Jesus smoke? Would Jesus drink beer? If you do not think that Jesus would do these things, and you profess to be his disciple, neither should you do them.

Conclusion

Jesus summed up these aspects of discipleship when he said, "If ye continue in my word, then are ye my disciples indeed; and ye shall know the truth, and the truth shall make you free" (Jn. 8:31-32). If you profess to be a disciple of Christ, you need to be involved in some kind of regular, systematic study of his revelation, you must adhere to the principles revealed therein, and be an imitator of Jesus who revealed God's word to us. If you are a Christian, you are a disciple. Are you a disciple?

Questions
True or False
_____ 1. The word "disciple" implies that one is a learner from a teacher.
_____ 2. Every disciple is an apostle.
_____ 3. Every apostle is a disciple.
_____ 4. Some Christians are not disciples.
_____ 5. A man can be a disciple of Christ without agreeing 100% with everything Jesus taught.

Matching
_____ 1. The disciples were called Christians.   a.   Matt. 28:18-20

____ 2. One must abide in Jesus' word to   b.   Acts 11:26
       be a disciple.
____ 3. A disciple is a follower of Jesus.   c.   Jn. 6:44-45
____ 4. Jesus has all authority over his disciples.   d.   Matt. 16:24
____ 5. One can become a disciple of Jesus only   e.   Jn. 8:31-32
       by learning of him.

Short Answer

1. Where were disciples first called Christians (Acts 11:26)? _____
_____

2. How does one become a disciple of Christ (Matt. 28:18-20)?_____
_____

3. How much authority over our lives should Jesus have (Matt. 28:18)? ___
_____

4. Why is Jesus qualified to teach us about God (Jn. 14:9; 12:45; 1:1)? _____
_____

5. Why should Christians study their Bible:
    a.   Heb. 5:11-14 _____
    b.   Eph. 5:14 _____
    c.   2 Pet. 2:1-2 _____

Jesus: The Master Teacher

1. What can man know about these subjects by human reasoning alone?
    a.   Existence of God? _____
    b.   Nature of God? _____
    c.   Number of gods? _____
    d.   Does man have a soul? _____
    e.   Is the soul immortal? _____
    f.   What must I do to be saved? _____
    g.   Is there a resurrection? _____
    h.   Heaven? _____
    i.   Hell? _____
2. What can we know about these same subjects through revelation?
    a.   Existence of God (Rom. 1:20; Psa. 19:1)? _____
_____
    b.   Nature of God (Exod. 34:6-7; Jn. 14:9)? _____
_____
    c.   Number of gods (1 Cor. 8:4)? _____
    d.   Does man have a soul (Matt. 10:28)? _____
    e.   Is the soul immortal (Matt. 10:28; 2 Cor. 4:16-5:10)? _____
_____
    f.   What must I do to be saved (Matt. 28:18-20; Mk. 16:15-16)? _____
_____

g. Is there a resurrection (Jn. 5:28-29)? _____

_____

h. Heaven (Jn. 14:1-3; Rev. 21)? _____

_____

i. Hell (Mk. 9:43-48)? _____

_____

Whose Disciple Are You?

In the chart below, fill out what the world says about the various subjects, not what Jesus says, and then tell who you follow:

Subject	World	Jesus	Whom I Follow
Fornication		1 Cor. 6:12-20	
Dress		1 Tim. 2:9-10	
Drinking		Prov. 20:1; 23:29f	
Language		James 3:1-12	

What Example Did Jesus Leave?

1. Regarding how to treat one's enemies (Matt. 5:43-48; Lk. 23:34)? _____

_____

2. Regarding forgiving others (Matt. 6:14-15)? _____

_____

3. Regarding how to deal with false teachers (Matt. 23)? _____

_____

4. Regarding how to resist sin (Matt. 4:1-11)? _____

_____

5. Regarding submitting to God's will (Matt. 26:39)? _____

_____

6. Regarding brotherly love (Jn. 13:34; 15:13)? _____

_____

7. Regarding moral purity (Heb. 4:15)? _____

_____

A Christian Is . . . A Servant

Perhaps individual personal freedom has as much importance to the American people as it does for any social group. Having an ancestry which has passed down to us accounts of the Boston Tea Party, the American Revolution, the Civil War, and World Wars I and II, Americans find the very mention of servitude and slavery repugnant. Personal liberty is valued highly. Slavery and human subjection to tyranny are the opposites of life, liberty and the pursuit of happiness presented as "inalienable rights" in the "Preamble" to the *Constitution of the United States.*

However much we might feel repugnant toward slavery, we must recognize that the Christian is a slave, a servant of God. He is so referred to in a number of texts (cf. Rom. 1:1; Phil. 1:1; Tit. 1:1; 2 Tim. 2:24).

What Is A Slave?

The New Testament uses several different words which are translated servant. There is *misthios*, the hired servant (Lk. 15:17,19; Mk. 1:20); *therapon*, a special representative of another whether free or slave (Heb. 3:5); *oiketes*, a domestic house servant. The most frequently used word is *doulos*. The *doulos* is a "slave, bondman, man of servile condition" (Joseph H. Thayer, *Greek-English Lexicon of the New Testament*, p. 158).

A man cannot be a slave without having a lord. The opposite of the slave is the lord. The servant/lord relationship is illustrated well by the statement of the centurion in Luke 7:8 – "For I am also a man set under authority, having under me soldiers, and I say unto one, Go, and he goeth; and to another, Come, and he cometh; *and to my servant, Do this, and he doeth it*" This was the normal relationship between a master and a slave. Jesus recognized this and used this to describe what a Christian is.

Spiritual Use of "Slave"

Spiritually, every man is a slave to either Satan or Christ. Jesus said, "Whosoever committeth sin is the servant of sin" (Jn. 8:34). Paul added, "Know ye not, that to whom ye yield yourselves servants to obey, his servants ye are to whom ye obey; whether of sin unto death, or of obedience unto righteousness? But God be thanked, that ye were the servants of sin, but ye have obeyed from the heart that form of doctrine which was delivered you. Being then made free from sin, ye became the servants of righteousness" (Rom. 6:16-18).

Sin enslaves men (Jn. 8:34). Peter described false teachers who promised liberty but were "servants of corruption" (2 Pet. 2:19). "His own iniquities shall take the wicked himself, and he shall be holden with the cords of his sins" (Prov. 5:22). We have witnessed those enslaved to their passions and lusts. Some have become drug addicts, alcoholics, sex perverts, homosexuals, etc., all the while defending their right to participate in these vices in the name of "personal liberty." The sinner is under the dominion of his sin and a slave of the devil.

In bygone days, slaves were auctioned to the highest bidder and sold as chattel property. Jesus redeemed us from slavery to sin, purchasing us with his own blood. The Scriptures teach that we have been purchased by Christ (cf. 2 Pet. 2:1).

> What? Know ye not that your body is the temple of the Holy Ghost which is in you, which ye have of God, and ye are not your own? For ye are bought with a price: therefore glorify God in your body, and in your spirit, which are God's (1 Cor. 6:19, 20).

> Ye are bought with a price; be not ye the servants of men (1 Cor. 7:23).

> We are not free men, we are slaves purchased by the Lord Jesus Christ.

Becoming Christ's slave freed us from our former master's tyranny; we are "free from sin" (Rom. 6:18). Christians are "delivered" (Rom. 6:17) from the bondage of sin. "Sin shall not have dominion over you" (Rom. 6:14). The truth makes us "free" (Jn. 8:32). "If the Son therefore shall make you free, ye shall be free indeed" (Jn. 8:36). The freedom into which Christians are called is freedom from slavery to sin, not freedom from all spiritual law.

Great Principles Learned From "Servant"

1. We must obey our Lord. Even as the first century slave recognized the authority of his lord over his life ("do this, and he doeth it"), so also does the servant of Christ recognize the lordship of Jesus Christ (cf. Acts 2:36). Jesus said, "Why call ye me, Lord, Lord, and do not the things which I say?" (Lk. 6:46) Referring to Jesus as "Lord" obligates one to obey the commandments of Jesus (compare to calling a man "boss" but not doing what he orders). The man who will be saved is the man who "does the will" of the Lord (Matt. 7:21). The Christian, therefore, is a man with the attitude and disposition that he will obey every commandment of his Lord Jesus Christ. Once the Christian perceives that something is the Lord's commandment, he will obey it.

2. A Christian has only one master. Jesus emphasized that a servant cannot serve two masters when he said, "No man can serve two masters: for either he will hate the one, and love the other; or else he will hold to the one, and despise the other. Ye cannot serve God and mammon" (Matt. 6:24). The impossibility of serving two masters, God and mammon, was demonstrated in the case of the rich young ruler in Matthew 19:16-22.

Paul emphasized the impossibility of serving two masters by saying, "Ye are bought with a price; be not ye the servants of men" (1 Cor. 7:23). He said, "For do I now persuade men, or God? Or do I seek to please men? For if I yet pleased men, I should not be the servant of Christ" (Gal. 1:10). The Christian has resolved to serve Christ instead of men.

When conflicts come between serving men, pursuing wealth, or serving Christ, the Christian recognizes that Jesus is his Master. He rejects the service of men, regardless of what fortunes or popularity that may offer, to serve his one and only Lord.

3. The will of the Lord is more important than the will of the slave. In the days of slavery, a slave recognized that his wishes had to be fitted around the master's will (see Luke 17:8-10). If he desired to do anything, he had (a) to seek the approval of his master for doing it and (b) do it at a time convenient to his master. Many Christians have forgotten that they are slaves of Jesus Christ. Many are so wrapped up in their own pursuits that they never even ask if they are doing what the Master wills.

Many are engaged in activities which their Master does not approve. Many are involved in the works of the flesh expressly condemned by the Lord (Gal. 5:19-21). Fornication, adultery, lasciviousness, revelry, and such like are present among Christians. Some also are guilty of hatred, variance, emulations, wrath, strife, seditions, heresies, envyings, etc. A Christian is a person who will not participate in an activity not approved by his Lord.

Even when the activity is approved by his Lord, the Christian must subordinate his desire to participate in it to the will of his Master. A slave would never have been allowed to go fishing on a day that the master commanded him to work. Similarly, Christ's slave will not allow approved, but unessential, activities to take precedence over his duties to Christ. Some have taken jobs which interfere with the worship and service of their God. Some participate in recreational activities which prohibit them from assembling with the saints and participating in the work the church does. Many are like the ones mentioned by Paul, "For all seek their own, not the things which are Jesus Christ's" (Phil. 2:21).

4. The servant is occupied in his Master's work. No man ever bought a slave unless he had a job for that slave to do. We who are bought with a price also have an obligation to be involved in the Master's work (cf. Tit. 1:16; 2:14; 3:1, 8). We become great in the Master's kingdom by service (Matt. 20:28). Here are some works that Christians should be doing: (a) Bearing the fruit of the Spirit (Gal. 5:22-23); (b) Helping the poor and needy, especially among the household of faith (Gal. 6:10; Jas. 1:27); (c) Teaching the lost (2 Tim. 2:2); (d) Showing hospitality to one another (1 Pet. 5:9).

The Blessed Servant

The blessed servant is the servant who, knowing the Lord's will, is busy doing that will. In his parables designed to exhort men to "watch therefore: for ye know not what hour your Lord doth come" (Matt. 24:42), Jesus said,

> Who then is a faithful and wise servant, whom his lord hath made ruler over his household, to give them meat in due season? Blessed is that servant, whom his lord when he cometh shall find so doing. Verily I say unto you, That he shall make him ruler over all his goods. But and if that evil servant shall say in his heart, My lord delayeth his coming; and shall begin to smite his fellowservants, and to eat and drink with the drunken; the lord of that servant shall come in a day when he looketh not for him, and in an hour that he is not aware of, and shall cut him asunder and appoint him his portion with the hypocrites: there shall be weeping and gnashing of teeth (Matt. 24:45-51).

In Matthew 25, the Lord taught the Parable of the Talents. The five and two-talent men who served their lord well were blessed. The lord said, "Well done, thou good and faithful servant: thou hast been faithful over a few things, I will make thee ruler over many things: enter thou into the joy of thy lord" (25:21,23). The slothful one-talent servant was cursed: "Thou wicked and slothful servant. . . .Cast ye the unprofitable servant into outer darkness: there shall be weeping and gnashing of teeth" (Matt. 25:26,30).

Conclusion

Christians are men who are busy in the Lord's work, not pursuing their own selfish ambitions, pursuit of pleasure, and fleshly lusts. Their primary interest in life is to serve their Lord, to do his bidding. Indeed, they are slaves of Jesus. Are you Jesus' slave? If not, you are not a Christian.

Questions
Multiple Choice

_____ 1. A servant (a) has a lord, (b) does the will of his lord, (c) has been purchased by his lord, (d) all of the above, (e) none of the above.

_____ 2. The word "servant" is applied to (a) poor Christians, (b) wicked Christians, (c) all Christians.

_____ 3. Christians are "free" (a) from the guilt of sin, (b) from obligations to any master (c) from all social obligations of servitude, (d) from obligation to any spiritual law.

____ 4. A servant does what he wishes (a) all of the time, (b) none of the time, (c) when his desires conform to his master's will.
____ 5. Every man is (a) a slave of sin, (b) a slave of Jesus, (c) either *a* or *b*.

Short Answer

1. Define "servant" or "slave." _____
    _____

2. What characteristics of a slave were used by Jesus to teach what a Christian is? _____
    _____
    _____

3. What two masters are described in Romans 6:16-18? _____
    _____

4. How does sin enslave men (Jn. 8:34)? _____
    _____

5. How did Jesus become the owner of his slave (1 Cor. 6:19-20)?_____
    _____

6. What is the significance of Jesus' being our "Lord" (Acts 2:36; Lk. 6:46)?
    _____

7. What obligation does a servant have to obey his Master? _____
    _____

8. What is taught by the phrase "ye are not your own" in 1 Corinthians 6:19-20? _____
    _____

9. Why is serving two masters impossible (Matt. 6:24)? _____
    _____

10. What conflicts might one have who is trying to serve God and mammon?
    _____
    _____

11. What conflicts might one have who is trying to serve God and men? ____
    _____

12. What are some works which you be doing as Christ's servant? _____
    _____

13. What kind of servant is blessed by Jesus (Matt. 24:45-51; 25:21, 23)? __
    _____

14. What kind of servant is cursed by Jesus (Matt. 25:26, 30)? _____
    _____
    _____

What Should I Do?

1. A Christian is being transferred on his job to an area of the country where not church exists. He has three children (ages 9, 12, 15). What should he do? _____

2. A little league game is scheduled for Wednesday night at 7:00. A Christian parent has a 12 year old son in little league. What should he do?

   _____

3. A gospel preacher is working with a congregation with elders. He discovers that an elder has been guilty of drunkenness. He is afraid that he will lose his job if he preaches against drinking or confronts the elder. What should he do? _____

4. A Christian has been invited to go fishing on Sunday morning. What should he do? _____

5. A Christian is a member of a bowling league which bowls on Sunday night at 6:00. He cannot be at evening worship services and the bowling league. What should he do? _____

A Christian Is . . . A Saint

In the New Testament, the Christian is designated as a saint (1 Cor. 1:2; 2 Cor. 1:1; Eph. 1:1; etc.). The word is not frequently used to describe God's people, probably because of the influence of denominational concepts regarding what is a saint. The Roman Catholic Church began the process of "canonization" of saints in the ninth century.

> In the Roman Church this (canonization, mw) is done by the pope only, who, after the examination, "declares the person in question to have led a perfect life, and that God hath worked miracles at his intercession, either during his life or after his death, and that, consequently, he is worthy to be honored as a saint, which implies permission to exhibit his relics, to invoke him, and to celebrate mass and an office in his honor." . . . The worship of "canonized saints" is enjoined by the Council of Trent (McClintock and Strong, *Cyclopedia of Biblical, Theological, and Ecclesiastical Literature*, Vol. II, pp. 90-91).

In Catholic usage, no one can become a saint until at least fifty years after his death.

The Catholic usage is not the same as the New Testament usage. Paul wrote to the church at Corinth and called them "saints" (1 Cor. 1:2). He was not writing to the dead but to the living; he was not writing to perfect people as the reading of the book will manifest. Rather, every Christian is a saint (2 Thess. 1:10). W.E. Vine wrote under the heading "saint": "In the plural, as used of believers, it designates all such and is not applied merely to persons of exceptional holiness, or to those who, having died, were characterized by exceptional acts of saintliness" (*An Expository Dictionary of New Testament Words*, Vol. III, p. 315). Hence, the word "saint" is another term to be considered in studying what a Christian is.

A Saint Is Set Apart

The word "saint" is translated from *hagios*, a word taken from the *hagi*-word group. This word group is translated by these English words: holy, holiness, saint, sanctuary, sanctify, sanctification, hallow. The significance of this word group is this: "things which on account of some connection with God possess a certain distinction and claim to reverence" (Thayer, *A Greek-*

English Lexicon, p. 6). There are, therefore, these holy things: (a) a holy city (Matt. 4:5); (b) a holy place (Matt. 24:15); (c) holy ground (Acts 7:33); (d) holy mountain (2 Pet. 1:18). Each of these things were "holy" because they were somehow set apart to God. The Temple was a holy place set apart to the worship of God; it was not to be used for profane purposes (cf. Jesus' cleansing of the Temple in Jn. 2:13-22). All the furniture of the Temple was set apart in a similar fashion. The priests who served in the Temple were "holy unto the Lord" (Lev. 21:6) because they were set apart to his worship. In a similar fashion, the whole nation of Israel was holy, not in the sense of moral purity, but in the sense of being separated especially to God (Exod. 19:5,7; Deut. 7:6; Jer. 2:3).

When the word "saint" is applied to a Christian, the first implication from the word is that Christians are "set apart to the service of God." They are not common people; they are "a chosen race, a royal priesthood, a holy nation, a people for God's own possession" (1 Pet. 2:9). Everyone who has been obedient to Jesus Christ is a saint, a person set apart to God. Hence, a Christian is a person set apart to the service of God (cf. ". . . present your bodies a living sacrifice, holy, acceptable unto God, which is your reasonable service" [Rom. 12:1]); he belongs to God (cf. ". . . ye are not your own? For ye are bought with a price: therefore glorify God in your body, and in your spirit, which are God's" [1 Cor. 6:19,20]). He is devoted to the service of God.

One is "set apart" to the Lord when he is baptized into Christ. Paul described this process of being set apart in 1 Corinthians 6:9-11.

> Know ye not that the unrighteous shall not inherit the kingdom of God? Be not deceived: neither fornicators, nor idolaters, nor adulterers, nor effeminate, nor abusers of themselves with mankind, nor thieves, nor covetous, nor drunkards, nor revilers, nor extortioners, shall inherit the kingdom of God. And such were some of you: but ye are washed, but ye are *sanctified*, but ye are justified in the name of the Lord Jesus Christ, and by the Spirit of our God.

The person is "set apart" unto God when he is "washed" and "justified." One is washed, sanctified, and justified when he is baptized into Christ for the remission of his sins!

This sanctification occurs through the word of truth. Jesus exhorted, "Sanctify them through thy truth: thy word is truth" (Jn. 17:17). Sanctification occurs through the call of the gospel by the Spirit of God. ". . . God hath from the beginning chosen you to salvation through sanctification of the Spirit and belief of the truth: whereunto he called you by our gospel, to the obtaining of the glory of our Lord Jesus Christ" (2 Thess. 2:13,14). The gospel of Jesus Christ reveals God's work through Jesus to us. When we believe and obey that gospel, we are set apart or sanctified through the truth.

The Ethical Sense

R. C. Trench said, "But the thought lies very near, that what is set apart from the world and to God, should separate itself from the world's defilements, and should share in God's purity; and in this way *hagios* speedily acquires a moral significance" (*Synonyms of the New Testament*, pp. 331-332). He who is separated to God is commanded, "But as he which hath called you is holy, so be ye holy in all manner of conversation" (1 Pet. 1:15). Those who are set apart to God must live holy lives; hence, the word saint designates the moral character of the life which the Christian lives.

The process of changing from a life of sin to a life of holiness is called "sanctification." Sanctification refers to the process by which one eradicates evil from his life and incorporates righteousness in it. Thus, a saint is not only one who is set apart to Christ, but also is one who is living a morally pure life (not a sinlessly perfect life). Paul wrote, "For this is the will of God, even your sanctification" (1 Thess. 4:3). The author of Hebrews exhorts, "Follow peace with all men, and holiness, without which no man shall see the Lord" (12:14).

Consider these passages which emphasize the moral transformation which occurs in a Christian: Galatians 5:19-22; 1 John 2:15-17; Romans 12:1-2; Ephesians 4:17-32; Colossians 3:5-17; 1 Peter 4:1-3. A Christian is a person who is devoted to cleansing his life of every defilement of flesh and spirit (2 Cor. 7:1). He prays as did David, "Search me, O God, and know my heart: try me, and know my thoughts: and see if there be any wicked way in me, and lead me in the way everlasting" (Psa. 139:23-24).

How Sanctification Occurs

The doctrine of "sanctification" has been a subject of controversy among the denominations. Two particular denominational ideas need to be mentioned before demonstrating how Bible sanctification occurs.

The Calvinist Concept. In Calvinism, man inherits a corrupt and depraved heart by natural generation from Adam. From this inherited depravity, not only is man guilty before God, but also do all sins occur. Man commits sin because he has a depraved nature. Conversion does not remove the depraved spirit. Hence, in order for a man to live above sin, the Holy Spirit must personally indwell the body to overcome the influence of the depraved spirit. To prevent the believer's imperfections or sins causing him to be lost, the perfect obedience of Christ is transferred to the believer's account so that he can never fall from grace.

The Wesleyan Concept. The Methodist doctrine of John and Charles Wesley states that man is born with a depraved nature as also does the Calvinist. However, they believe that an instantaneous, second act of grace occurs whereby the depraved nature is sanctified and man is able to live above sin. A Wesleyan Methodist might declare that he has lived years without ever sinning.

Bible Sanctification. Sanctification does not occur through either of these processes. Jesus said, "Sanctify them through thy truth: thy word is truth" (Jn. 17:17). In what way is sanctification related to the word? The word of God is related to sanctification in the moral sense in the same fashion as it is related to sanctification in the sense of conversion. A person is set apart to God through conversion when he hears the gospel and obeys it (Jas. 1:21; 1 Pet. 1:22-23; Jn. 6:44-45). One learns of God's will, believes it, and obeys it, causing him to be set apart to the Lord.

The process of moral purification works in the same way. Consider what Paul said concerning the Scriptures in 2 Timothy 3:16-17 – "All scripture is given by inspiration of God, and is profitable for doctrine, for reproof, for correction, for instruction in righteousness: that the man of God may be perfect, throughly furnished unto all good works." Notice what Scripture does: (a) *Reproof.* Reproof is the manner by which the person is convicted of the sinfulness of his conduct. (b) *Correction.* Correction is the restoration to an upright state. Thus, the Scriptures do not leave a person convicted of sin, they straighten him out. (c) *Instruction in righteousness.* Having demonstrated that the wrong manner of life must be corrected, the Scriptures also point the way to the right kind of living. The Scriptures do not stop with the "thou shalt not's"; they add the "thou shalt's."

Thus, the sanctification process is related to the Scriptures in this way. Through them we learn of our misconduct, the way to correct our lives, and the right way of life. Thus, the sanctification of the believer "is not vicarious, i.e., it cannot be transferred or imputed (as in the Calvinist doctrine of the imputation of the perfect obedience of Christ to the believer, mw), it is an individual possession, built up, little by little (it is not an instantaneous second work of grace, mw), as the result of obedience to the Word of God and of following the example of Christ" (W.E. Vine, *An Expository Dictionary of New Testament Words*, "Sanctification," Vol. III, p. 317).

Conclusion

The word "saint" then testifies to both the unique relationship sustained by the Christian to God as well as to the moral character which results from that association with God. Needless to say, many who call themselves Christians are not reflecting the moral character of a saint. Such a person is self-deceived if he believes that he can walk in the ways of the world and sustain a right relationship with God. Since a Christian is sanctified and in the process of sanctification, he can be called a saint! Are you a Christian?

Questions
Multiple Choice
____ 1. In Catholic teaching, a saint (a) has lived a perfect life, (b) has lived a good life, (c) is living a good life.
____ 2. In Catholic teaching, a saint is (a) someone to whom you can pray, (b) can be venerated or worshipped, (c) has answered prayer by performing miracles, (d) all of the above, (e) none of the above.
____ 3. In Catholic teaching, a saint has been dead (a) 10, (b) 50, (c) 100 years.
____ 4. Which passages shows that a saint is a believer? (a) Exod. 19:5-7; (b) 1 Pet. 2:9; (c) 2 Thess. 1:10
____ 5. Which passages shows that saints are alive? (a) 1 Cor. 1:2; (b) 2 Cor. 1:1; (c) Eph. 1:1; (d) all of the above; (e) none of the above.
____ 6. In the Calvinist concept of sanctification, man inherits a corrupt nature from Adam but this can be overcome by (a) extra-ordinary human effort, (b) prayer, (c) the personal indwelling of the Holy Spirit.
____ 7. In Calvinist thought, a Christian cannot fall from grace because (a) the perfect obedience of Christ is transferred to him, (b) he never sins.
____ 8. In Wesleyan or Methodist doctrine, sanctification occurs (a) over a long period of time, (b) instantly by a second work of grace.
____ 9. A person who has received the second work of grace (a) lives above sin, (b) no longer has a depraved nature, (c) both of the above, (d) neither of the above.

Matching
____ 1. Holy city
____ 2. Holy anointing oil
____ 3. Holy place (Temple)
____ 4. Holy ground
____ 5. Holy mountain

a. Exod. 30:31
b. 2 Pet. 1:18
c. Matt. 4:5
d. Acts 7:33
e. Matt. 24:15

What made each of these items "holy"? _____
_____

Short Answer
1. In what sense is a Christian "set apart" (1 Pet. 2:9)? _____
_____

2. In what way does a Christian "belong" to God (1 Cor. 6:19, 20)? _____
_____

3. When is the sinner "set apart" (1 Cor. 6:9-11)? _____
_____

4. How does the word of God cause this sanctification (Jn. 17:17)? _____
_____

5. Why does "sanctify" shift in meaning to include "moral purity" (1 Pet. 1:15)? _____

_____

6. What attitude should a person have toward attaining moral purity (Psa. 139:23-24)? _____

_____

7. From 2 Timothy 3:16,17, define the role of Scripture in sanctification by defining these terms:
    a. Reproof: _____
    b. Correction: _____
    c. Instruction in righteousness: _____
8. What do Romans 3:20 and 7:7 say the role of Scripture is in bringing us to moral purity? _____

_____

9. What role does Psalm 119:9-11 attribute to the word of God in sanctification? _____

_____

10. How does Ephesians 4:22-23 describe the moral change in a Christian?

_____

_____

11. Study Ephesians 4:25-32. How does being a Christian affect one's:
    a. Speech (4:25,26,29,31)? _____

    _____

    b. Anger (4:26-27)? _____
    c. Manner of providing for himself (4:28)? _____

    _____

    d. Use of his money (4:28)? _____
    e. Conduct toward others (4:31-32)? _____

    _____

12. What does sanctification require in 1 Thessalonians 4:3-7?_____

_____

13. Name some modern sins that are sometimes tolerated by Christians but that are inconsistent with his being a saint. _____

_____

_____

14. If being a Christian is being a saint, is one a Christian if he does not live like a saint? _____

_____

A Christian Is . . . A Pilgrim, Sojourner, Or Stranger

Peter wrote, "Dearly beloved, I beseech you as strangers and pilgrims, abstain from fleshly lusts, which war against the soul" (1 Pet. 2:11). On several occasions, the New Testament uses the words "stranger," "sojourner," and "pilgrim" as descriptive names for Christians.

For many of us, "pilgrim" stirs in our minds the memory of the Pilgrim fathers of our country who founded Plymouth Colony in 1620. Some may also associate the idea with "pilgrimage," taking a journey to some distant holy place. Neither of these uses captures the New Testament meaning of the word.

What Is A Pilgrim, Stranger, or Sojourner?

The New Testament words for "pilgrim," "sojourner," and "stranger" cannot be understood without understanding the cultural background from which they were derived. The Hebrew verb *gur* means "sojourn. . . dwell for a (definite or indef.) time, dwell as a new-comer (cf. *ger*) without original rights" (Brown, Driver, and Briggs, *A Hebrew and English Lexicon of the Old Testament*, p. 157). The noun *ger* means "sojourner . . . temporary dweller, new-comer (no inherited rights)" (*Ibid.* p. 158). These words are used to describe Abraham's stay in Egypt (Gen. 12:10), where he fled to escape the effects of the famine in Canaan. He was not a citizen of Egypt; rather, he was an alien residing in a foreign country. Lot's stay in Sodom (Gen. 19:9) and a non-citizen dwelling in a foreign country are other examples of the use of this word (Exod. 12:48-49). An alien residing in a land was without rights in the land in which he dwelt.

The New Testament has this same use. Thayer defines *parepidemos* to mean "prop. one who comes from a foreign country into a city or land to reside there by the side of the natives; hence, stranger, sojourning in a strange place, a foreigner, . . . in the N.T. metaph. in ref. to heaven as the native country, one who sojourns on earth; so of Christians in 1 Pet. i.1" (*Greek-English Lexicon of the New Testament*, p. 488). The word is used in Acts 2:10 to describe the Jews from Rome who were residing in Jerusalem and in Acts 17:21 to denote visitors to the city of Athens.

The word *paroikos* has this similar definition: "1. in class. Grk. dwelling near, neighboring. 2. in the Scriptures, a stranger, foreigner, one who lives in a place without the right of citizenship" (*Ibid.*, p. 490). It is used of the patriarchs' sojourn in Canaan, a land in which they had no citizenship (Acts 7:6; Heb. 11:9). Israel's stay in Egypt for 400 years was a sojourn (Acts 13:17), inasmuch as that was not their permanent home.

We can understand what a "stranger," "pilgrim," or "sojourner" is by thinking of soldiers being assigned to a two year tour of duty in a foreign country. The soldiers recognize that they will be in that country for a short period of time. They make little effort to learn its language, customs, and people. They do not try to establish themselves financially in the society by buying property and entering business. They count the days until their tour is over, yearning for the time of their return to their homeland. This is the idea that is emphasized when Peter says that Christians are "pilgrims," "sojourners," and "strangers."

William Barclay captured the idea in these comments on Ephesians 2:19:

> Paul used the word *xenos* for foreigner. In every Greek city there were *xenoi*, and their life was not easy. A man who was a stranger in a strange city writes home, "It is better for you to be in your homes, whatever they may be like, than to be in a strange land." The foreigner was always regarded with suspicion and dislike. Paul used the word *paroikos* for sojourner. The *paroikos* was one step further on. He was a resident alien; he was a man who had come to stay in a place but who had never become a naturalized citizen; he paid a tax for the privilege of existing in a land which was not his own. He might stay there and he might work there, but he was a stranger and an outsider whose home was somewhere else. Both the *xenos* and *paroikos* were where thy were on sufferance; they were always on the fringe (*The Letters to the Galatians and Ephesians*, p. 138).

Our Citizenship Is In Heaven

The true citizenship of the Christian is not citizenship in an earthly kingdom, but citizenship in an eternal kingdom. Paul wrote, "For our citizenship is in heaven, from which also we eagerly wait for a Savior, the Lord Jesus Christ" (Phil. 3:20, NASB). We are strangers and sojourners on this earth, i.e., we are resident aliens, non-citizens. Jacob described his life as a pilgrimage when he stood before Pharaoh (Gen. 47:9). The idea of the sojourning of the Patriarchs is discussed in Hebrews 11:8-16.

> By faith Abraham, when he was called to go out into a place when he should after receive for an inheritance, obeyed; and he went out, not knowing whither he went. By faith he sojourned in the land of promise, as in a strange country,

dwelling in tabernacles with Isaac and Jacob, the heirs with him of the same promise: for he looked for a city which hath foundations, whose builder and maker is God. . . . These all died in faith, not having received the promises, but having seen them afar off, and were persuaded of them, and embraced them, and confessed that they were strangers and pilgrims on the earth. For they that say such things declare plainly that they seek a country. And truly, if they had been mindful of that country from whence they came out, they might have had opportunity to have returned. But now they desire a better country, that is, an heavenly: wherefore God is not ashamed to be called their God: for he hath prepared for them a city.

We who are Christians must develop the same attitude toward our lives as the patriarchs had. "For here have we no continuing city, but we seek one to come" (Heb. 13:14).

We are strangers and sojourners on this earth. Our citizenship is in heaven. We sing this message in this song:

This World Is Not My Home

This world is not my home, I'm just a passing through.
My treasures are laid up somewhere beyond the blue.
The angels beckon me from heaven's open door,
And I can't feel at home in this world anymore.

O Lord, you know I have no friend like you,
If heaven's not my home, then Lord what will I do?
The angels beckon me from heaven's open door,
And I can't feel at home in this world anymore.

– Albert E. Brumley

Heavenly Citizenship Is Available To All

A new idea for the New Testament age was that all men could be citizens in the Lord's kingdom. Paul spoke of the conversion of the Gentiles when he wrote, "Now therefore ye are no more strangers and foreigners, but fellow-citizens with the saints, and of the household of God" (Eph. 2:19). Earlier Paul had declared that Gentiles were separate from Christ, excluded from the commonwealth of Israel, strangers to the covenants of promise, having no hope, and without God in this world (Eph. 2:12). However, through Christ, Gentiles are made part of the kingdom of God. They are not second-class citizens in the kingdom but participate with full citizenship rights with the Jews in the Lord's kingdom. Hence, the gospel provides citizenship privileges to all of mankind. To become a citizen in the kingdom, a person must be born again (Jn. 3:3,5).

Effects on One's Life

When one recognizes himself to be a pilgrim and sojourner, his attitude and dispositions toward life will be as definitely affected as are the attitudes on the soldier stationed on foreign soil. Here are some effects this will have:

1. He will set his mind on heavenly things. Because my citizenship is in heaven, not on earth, I will not set my affections on things of this earth (Col. 3:1-2). How many goods I accumulate is relatively unimportant inasmuch as I must leave all of them behind. Keeping up with the Jones' of society is insignificant. Whether I conform to the fashions of this world makes little difference (cf. to whether a soldier stationed in a foreign country is very concerned with whether or not he dresses according to the latest fashions of the country in which he is stationed). What is more important is being sure that I make it home to where my citizenship is – to heaven.

Inasmuch as his treasure is in heaven, he will meditate and think about heaven frequently. David confessed, "Thy statutes have been my songs in the house of my pilgrimage" (Psa. 119:54). "I am a stranger in the earth: hide not thy commandments from me" (Psa. 119:19). Do your thoughts dwell on eternal things?

2. He will avoid any entanglement that might hamper his attaining his heavenly home (2 Tim. 2:4). One's disposition must be, "Reaching heaven is life's most important goal. I will do nothing that interferes with attaining that goal." This attitude is sometimes displayed by worldly people who seek some earthly goal. I listened one day to a radio interview with a movie star who was giving advice to young people about how to become a movie star. The star commented about how slim a chance an individual has to make it to stardom and, therefore, advised anyone aspiring to become a movie star to get a good paying job. Then, the individual should take a job and work at it, taking studio performances as they came. Then, she advised that, if an opportunity to perform should present itself, however small the role might be (one never knows what might be just the break he needs), take it, even if it means giving up the job which the person has. The reasoning behind this advice was as follows: Your primary goal is to reach stardom; always keep that first in importance; make everything fit around it. This is exactly the attitude a Christian should have toward attaining heaven. My service to God is the most important part of my life; everything else – jobs, recreation, house, car, etc. – must be fitted around that goal.

Having this attitude makes many of life's decisions easier for the Christian. When looking for a job, a Christian should ask, "How will this job affect my being a Christian? Will I be able to worship regularly? Will I be in a wholesome atmosphere? Can I handle the temptations which I must face?" A relative of mine was offered a promotion and a raise in pay if he would relocate in a city in which no faithful congregation existed. He moved there and then cried for help saying, "What am I going to do? There is no faithful church within driving distance." He knew that he was expected to worship God before he took that job. He should have thought about these problems before he moved there. I heard a preacher once say, "If your job interferes with your service as a Christian, quit it. I'll guarantee you that you will get a better job." Before you become critical of our brother for promising things which he cannot guarantee will occur, I should add that he said, "Oh, it might not pay as much but it will be a better job!" A job in which one can faithfully serve God is better than a job that conflicts with one's service to God, regardless of the pay differential.

When deciding upon recreational activities, a Christian will ask, "Can I participate in this activity and go to heaven when I die? Is it interfering with my service to God? Will I have to miss worship in order to participate?"

A Christian can truly sing the words of the song "Here We Are But Straying Pilgrims" by I.N. Carman. Can you sing these words?

> Here we are but straying pilgrims;
> Here our path is often dim;
> But to cheer us on our journey,
> Still we sing this wayside hymn:
>
> Yonder over the rolling river,
> Where the shining mansions rise,
> Soon will be our home forever,
> And the smile of the blessed Giver
> Gladdens all our longing eyes.
>
> Here our feet are often weary
> On the hills that throng our way;
> Here the tempest darkly gathers,
> But our hearts within us say:
>
> Yonder over the rolling river,
> Where the shining mansions rise,
> Soon will be our home forever,
> And the smile of the blessed Giver
> Gladdens all our longing eyes.
>
> Here our souls are often fearful
> Of the pilgrim's lurking foe;
> But the Lord is our defender,
> And he tells us we may know:
>
> Yonder over the rolling river,
> Where the shining mansions rise,
> Soon will be our home forever,
> And the smile of the blessed Giver
> Gladdens all our longing eyes.

Questions
Matching

_____ 1. 1 Peter 1:1   a. The patriarchs confessed themselves
                                            to be strangers and pilgrims.
_____ 2. Acts 17:21   b. Christians are called "strangers."
_____ 3. Hebrews 11:13   c. Abram sojourned in Egypt to escape the
                                            famine.
_____ 4. 1 Peter 2:11   d. Christians are known as "pilgrims."
_____ 5. Genesis 12:10   e. Aliens residing in Athens.

Short Answer

1. What is a "pilgrim," "sojourner," or "stranger"? _____
    _____
    _____

2. In a spiritual sense, where is a Christian's citizenship (Phil. 3:20)? _____

3. Where is a Christian's place of residence? _____
    _____

4. From Hebrews 11:8-16, answer these questions:
    a. In what land had Abraham had citizenship? _____
    b. In what land was he a sojourner? _____
    c. What city became the place of his citizenship (vv. 10, 15-16)? _____
        _____
    d. Why was God not ashamed to be called the "God of Abraham, Isaac,
        and Jacob" (v. 16)? _____
        _____

5. Who can become citizens in the kingdom of God (cf. Eph. 2:19)? _____
    _____

6. How does one become a citizen in the kingdom of God (Jn. 3:5)? _____
    _____

7. What effect does the recognition that one's citizenship is in heaven have
    on:
    a. One's affections (Col. 3:1-2)? _____
        _____
    b. One's choice of a job? _____
        _____
    c. One's involvement in recreation? _____
        _____

Decisions, Decisions

How would recognition that one is a pilgrim or sojourner affect these situations?

1. A teenager is being mocked because he does not join in telling filthy

jokes, drinking, etc. _____
_____
_____
_____

2. A Christian is being pressured to do things on his job that are wrong (lie about his product, entertain clients with alcoholic beverages, etc.).
_____
_____
_____

3. A recreational activity in which a Christian is involved is scheduled so that it conflicts with worship services. _____
_____
_____

Lesson 7

A Christian Is . . . A Steward

The apostle Peter wrote, "As every man hath received the gift, even so minister the same one to another, as good *stewards* of the manifold grace of God" (1 Pet. 4:10). "For the bishop must be blameless, as the *steward* of God" (Tit. 1:7). In our consideration of what a Christian is, we must remember that a Christian is a steward of those things entrusted to him.

What Is A Steward?

The word "steward" is rarely used in English because the practice of employing stewards is obsolete; indeed, whenever one is put in a position similar to a steward, we give him another title, such as "manager." The word "steward" (*oikonomos*) is defined by Joseph Henry Thayer as follows: "the manager of a household or of household affairs; esp. a steward, manager, superintendent . . . to whom the head of a house or proprietor has intrusted the management of his affairs, the care of receipts and expenditures, and the duty of dealing out the proper portion to every servant and even to the children not yet of age" (*A Greek-English Lexicon*, pp. 440-441).

The practice of using stewards is portrayed in several Bible examples. Joseph served the role of a steward to Potiphar (Gen. 39:4). The parable of the unjust steward (Lk. 16:1-12) reflects the practice of stewardship. The master of the parable had entrusted his goods to the steward, expecting him to use them profitably in his absence.

When we consider the practice of stewardship and make the spiritual application to us as Christians, we can understand why we are called stewards. Here are some reasons: *(1) God owns everything* that *He has created.* We must look upon everything we have as that which belongs to God; "for the earth is the Lord's, and the fulness thereof" (1 Cor. 10:26). *(2) Men are using that which belongs to God.* We do not own anything; we are only using that which belongs to God. The land that we "own" will be here long after we are dead and gone; our money will be left to our heirs. *(3) We are responsible for how we use the things which God has given to us.* The very fact that we are stewards implies that we oversee the use of God's possessions. We can use them either properly (that is, as the owner thereof has directed) or improperly (that is, squandering them on our own pleasures). We have freedom of choice. However, you must never forget that we must "give account of thy stewardship" (Lk. 16:2). J. G. Small expressed the concept of stewardship in the song "I've Found A Friend." He wrote,

> I've found a Friend, O, such a Friend!
> He bled, He died to save me;
> And not alone the gift of life,
> But His own self He gave me.
>
> Naught that I have my own I call,
> I hold it for the Giver;
> My heart, my strength, my life, my all,
> Are His, and His forever.

Areas of Responsibility

1. Our abilities. God has endowed each person with certain natural abilities for which he will be held responsible. This was the idea that prompted Paul to write, "For though I preach the gospel, I have nothing to glory of: for necessity is laid upon me; yea, woe is unto me, if I preach not the gospel!" (1 Cor. 9:16). The parable of the talents shows that responsibility is related to one's ability: "And unto one he gave five talents, to another two, and to another one; to every man according to his several ability" (Matt. 25:15). God has given me certain abilities for which he will hold me responsible.

Many brethren exercise a double standard with reference to the idea of stewardship of abilities. For example, not a few who would be critical of a preacher should he decide to quit preaching feel no responsibility to develop their own abilities. The same principle which says that I should preach, if I have the ability to preach, implies that every other person who has the ability to preach should develop his abilities so that he can preach. Furthermore, the principle says that, if you have the ability to teach a class, lead singing, make announcements, clean the church building, prepare the Lord's supper, mow the yard, etc., you have a responsibility to do that. Every person must look upon his inherited abilities as a stewardship to use them in God's service. The church functions as every individual does his part, using the abilities which God has given him in God's service (1 Cor. 12:12-21; Eph. 4:16).

2. Our time. Even as we are responsible for the proper use of our abilities, so also are we responsible for the use of our time. Paul wrote, "See then that ye walk circumspectly, not as fools, but as wise, redeeming the time, because the days are evil" (Eph. 5:15-16; Col. 4:5). Frequently, when asked to do something, we excuse ourselves by saying, "I do not have the time to do it." Some "do not have the time" to attend worship, study the Bible, check on the sick, or do any other of the responsibilities God has placed upon them. Nevertheless, they have time to watch TV, go to ball games, watch TV, go out to eat, and watch TV. The problem is not that the man does not have the time to do anything for the Lord; the problem is that God is not one of his top priorities. He has squandered the time that God has entrusted to him on his own selfish pleasures (cf. 2 Tim. 4:4; Phil. 3:19). The psalmist wrote, "So teach us to number our days, that we may apply our hearts unto wisdom" (Psa. 90:12).

3. Our wealth. Both the wealth which we have and the ability to make it come from the Lord (Hag. 2:8; Deut. 8:18). God has simply entrusted the use of our money to us. For a brother who makes a good salary to contribute a mere $10 per week to the Lord is not uncommon. Such a use of money reflects an improper attitude toward wealth.

Christians should not be treasuring up money on earth (cf. Matt. 6:19-34). Some have that attitude. They are "minded to be rich" (cf. 1 Tim. 6:9-10, 17-19). They have more concern for saving for the future than for giving to the Lord today (cf. Matt. 6:34; Lk. 12:15-21). We should be using the gift of prosperity which we have received from the Lord for these purposes (in addition to providing for our own): (a) helping the needy (Gal. 2:10; 6:10; Jas. 1:27; Acts 2:44-45; 4:35-37) and (b) supporting the preaching of the gospel (Gal. 6:6; Phil. 4:15-17; 1 Cor. 9:1-15; 16:1-2; 9:6ff).

Some bring their scraps to the Lord. After they obligate themselves to all kinds of bills and spend on their selfish pleasures, then they take out of their leftovers a donation for the Lord. The Christian does not so use his money. The Lord receives the "firstfruits" of his prosperity.

4. The gospel. One of the Lord's richest treasures, the gospel of Christ, has been entrusted to us. Paul said, "Let a man so account of us, as of the ministers of Christ, and stewards of the mysteries of God. Moreover, it is required in stewards, that a man be found faithful" (1 Cor. 4:1-2). Here are some responsibilities that we have: (a) To pass the word down intact to the next generation. "Hold fast the form of sound words, which thou hast heard of me, in faith and love which is in Christ Jesus. That good thing which was committed unto thee keep by the Holy Ghost which dwelleth in us" (2 Tim. 1:13-14). (b) To preach it to a lost world. My responsibility is to take the gospel to those who are living in sin (2 Tim. 2:2; Matt. 28:18-20). Why are so many of us content when the world around us dies without knowing the gospel of Christ? Paul wrote his thoughts about this responsibility, "Unto me, who am less than the least of all saints, is this grace given, that I should preach among the Gentiles the unsearchable riches of Christ" (Eph. 3:8). (c) To preach all the gospel. "I am pure from the blood of all men. For I have not shunned to declare unto you all the counsel of God" (Acts 20:26-27; cf. 1 Thess. 2:4). I dare not fail to teach something that men need to hear because of fear of some rejection or persecution.

5. My children. Children are a heritage from the Lord (Psa. 127:3). God has entrusted parents with the task of bringing up their children in the nurture and admonition of the Lord (Eph. 6:4), to teach them God's word (Deut. 6:6-7; Psa. 78:5-6). Children come to us from the hand of God; he has entrusted them to our care, holding us responsible for teaching them his word. A child left to himself will bring shame to his parents (Prov. 29:15). My responsibility is to teach my children the word of God, providing them the training they need to function in society, business, government, and worship.

Conclusion

Every steward must give account of his stewardship. The parable of the unfaithful steward (Lk. 16:1-15) tells of a steward who abused the goods entrusted to him. He was afraid when the time came to give account of his stewardship. The parable of the talents describes the one-talent servant who did not use his master's goods in his service (Matt. 25:14-30). There is coming a day in which each of us will give account of his use of his goods in God's service. Have you been a good steward of God's gifts?

Questions

1. What is a steward? _____

_____

2. How are Christians compared to stewards? _____

_____

3. What extra-ordinary abilities do you have? _____

_____

4. How might you use them in God's service? _____

_____

5. How have you tried to develop your natural abilities to use them in God's service? _____

_____

6. What is the condition of one who does not use his abilities in God's service (1 Cor. 9:16; Matt. 25:14-30)? _____

_____

7. How many hours do you spend on the following each week?
    a. Hours at work? _____
    b. Hours sleeping? _____
    c. Hours eating? _____
    d. Hours watching TV? _____
    e. Hours in other recreational activities? _____
    f. Hours in spiritual activities? _____

8. Why is "I don't have the time" an unacceptable excuse for not doing what God commanded (Eph. 5:15-16; Col. 4:5)? _____
    _____

9. Why might a person "not have the time" to do what God commands (2 Tim. 4:4; Phil. 3:9)? _____
    _____

10. If you analyzed your income, what percentage do you spend for:
    a. Housing (utilities, payments, etc.)? _____
    b. Food? _____
    c. Recreational? _____
    d. Savings? _____
    e. Transportation? _____
    f. Contribution? _____
11. Could you survive on 10 times what you give to the Lord?_____
    _____

12. What wrong uses of one's prosperity may cause him not to give as he should? _____
    _____

13. How might one be giving his "scraps" to the Lord? _____
    _____

14. What responsibility do we have to the next generation in passing down the gospel (2 Tim. 1:13-14)? _____
    _____

15. What responsibility do we have to the lost (2 Tim. 2:2)? _____
    _____

16. What responsibility does a parent have to his children as a steward of God (Deut. 6:6-7; Psa. 78:5-6)? _____
    _____

17. How many years do I have to accomplish this stewardship?_____
    _____

18. What happens to the parents of the child who was not properly trained (Prov. 29:15)? _____
    _____

A Christian Is . . . A Soldier

Paul referred to Epaphroditus and Archippus as his "fellow-soldiers" (Phil. 2:25; Phile. 2). The language of Paul's charges to Timothy is full of military imagery.

> This charge I commit unto thee, son Timothy, according to the prophecies which went before on thee, that thou by them mightest war a good warfare (1 Tim. 1:18).

> Fight the good fight of faith, lay hold on eternal life, whereunto thou art also called, and hast professed a good profession before many witnesses (1 Tim. 6:12).

> Thou therefore endure hardness, as a good soldier of Jesus Christ. No man that warreth entangleth himself with the affairs of this life; that he may please him who had chosen him to be a soldier (2 Tim. 2:3,4).

> I have fought a good fight, I have finished my course, I have kept the faith (2 Tim. 4:7).

A Christian is a soldier of Christ. What aspects of being a Christian are revealed through this comparison?

The Christian Is At War

Being a Christian means that we are engaged in a great spiritual warfare – a battle between Christ and the Devil – in which we serve as soldiers fighting against the Devil's army. The book of Revelation lifts the curtain so that we can see the present conflict between Christ and Satan. John told of his vision, "And the dragon was wroth with the woman, and went to make war with the remnant of her seed, which keep the commandments of God, and have the testimony of Jesus Christ" (Rev. 12:17). The conflict will have a decisive battle: "And I saw the beast, and the kings of the earth, and their armies, gathered together to make war against him that sat on the horse (Jesus, mw), and against his army" (Rev. 19:19). Christians should recognize that they are soldiers of Christ in war against the army of the Devil.

Ours is a spiritual conflict. "For we wrestle not against flesh and blood, but against principalities, against powers, against the rulers of the darkness of this world, against spiritual wickedness in high places" (Eph. 6:12). The battle is not like earthly wars for possession of earthly terrain. Jesus said, "My kingdom is not of this world: if my kingdom were of this world, then would my servants fight, that I should not be delivered to the Jews: but now is my kingdom not from hence" (Jn. 18:36). In the Middle Ages, people misunderstood the nature of the kingdom as they sent Crusades to defeat the Muslims to gain control of the Bible lands. That is not the nature of the conflict in which we are engaged.

We do not use carnal weapons. "For the weapons of our warfare are not carnal, but mighty through God to the pulling down of strong holds; casting down imaginations, and every high thing that exalteth itself against the knowledge of God, and bringing into captivity every thought to the obedience of Christ" (2 Cor. 10:3-4). A Christian realizes this battle is occurring and fights with the sword of the Spirit to bring victory to Christ.

Though the warfare is spiritual, the enemy is nonetheless real. Satan is not the figment of one's imagination; he is not a mythological creature. He goes about as a roaring lion seeking whom he may devour (1 Pet. 4:8). He sifts souls like wheat (Lk. 22:31). The book of Job reveals the activity of Satan in trying to destroy and capture Job's soul. He is unscrupulous in his assaults against the soul (note: the "wiles of the devil," Eph. 6:11). Here are some of his tactics: (a) mixes truth and error (Gen. 3:4, 5, 22), (b) misquotes Scripture (Matt. 4:6), (c) masquerades as an angel of light (2 Cor. 11:14), (d) promises that good may come through the practice of evil (Lk. 4:6-7), (e) appeals to the body's physical desires (Jas. 4:1; 1 Pet. 2:11). He is not an honorable enemy.

Soldiers of Christ must join in the fray. The mouths of false teachers must be stopped (Tit. 1:11), sinners must be rebuked (1 Tim. 5:20; Eph. 5:11). Men must be set for the defense of the gospel (Phil. 1:17). These are not pleasant tasks, but they are tasks which soldiers of Christ must perform. Sometimes men do harm to the war effort by criticizing their fellow soldiers when he assaults Satan's army. A gospel preacher may do the work of exposing the false doctrines of a false teacher who is leading men into sin and damnation. When this happens, someone writes something like this:

> By our obnoxious name-calling, negative fault-finding spirits and "McCarthyisms," we have run off everyone who might be interested in filling their spiritual needs. . . . I am discouraged over gospel preachers who spend their time trying to ruin the reputations of other good gospel preachers because of personal jealousies and envies. . . . We have "issues" which brethren have simply drummed up because they do not like other brethren, and they seek to hang every other thing on such issues. . . . We have become too busy "standing

firm" instead of teaching the lost. We are too busy talking about our negative, back-biting view of Christianity to ever present it in a way that would demonstrate the love of God for the lost world.

No one defends obnoxious name calling, negative fault-finding, personal attacks motivated by jealousy and envy, or backbiting. However, one would be naive to ignore the fact that some are unwilling to kindly, forthrightly and sincerely repudiate false doctrine and name the man who is teaching it. They cannot conceive of doing battle in this manner with sin and error. Doing this is beneath their dignity. Such writing as that above undermines the work of the good soldiers of Christ who are contending for the faith (Jude 3). Let us never be guilty of lending support to the enemy by attacking the soldiers of Christ when they are doing the work of a good soldier.

Preparation for Battle

The soldier of Christ needs to be prepared to do battle. Here is the Christian's armor:

> Put on the whole armor of God, that ye may be able to stand against the wiles of the devil. . . . Wherefore take unto you the whole armor of God, that ye may be able to withstand in the evil day, and having done all, to stand. Stand therefore, having your loins girt about with truth, and having on the breastplate of righteousness; and your feet shod with the preparation of the gospel of peace; above all, taking the shield of faith, wherewith ye shall be able to quench all the fiery darts of the wicked. And take the helmet of salvation, and the sword of the Spirit, which is the word of God: praying always with all prayer and supplication in the Spirit. . . (Eph. 6:11, 13-18).

This passage instructs us in withstanding the assaults of the devil. Hence, the Christian's armor must be understood from the perspective of what is necessary to stay faithful to Christ. The articles of the armor are as follows:

1. *"Your loins girt about with truth."* The truth in this passage is not the gospel, the word of truth, for that is described as the sword of the Spirit. The truth seems to be one's personal integrity, his truthfulness (cf. Prov. 11:3). One armor that a Christian should always wear is integrity; he should not violate his own conscience; he should be true to what he knows is right. The first steps into sin compromise one's conscience, making subsequent acts of ungodliness easier. Keeping one's integrity is one safeguard against Satan.

2. *"The breastplate of righteousness."* This may be understood as "justification" or "acts of righteousness." The latter seems to be intended in this text. Those who are busy doing acts of righteousness are wearing an armor of protection against the devil's assaults. Christians busy in the Lord's work stay faithful.

3. *"Feet shod with the preparation of the gospel."* This points to evangelism.

Those who are busy spreading the word to their friends and neighbors are better protected against the temptations of the flesh than those who are not.

4. "The shield of faith." Faith refers to the Christian's personal faith in the revealed word of God. The temptation of Jesus demonstrates how his personal belief and trust in the revealed word of God sustained him in overcoming the assaults of the Devil (Matt. 4:1-11).

5. "The helmet of salvation." The hope of salvation serves as a protection to the mind. It is the anchor of the soul (Heb. 6:19-20). This living hope guards us from apostasy.

6. "The sword of the Spirit." The sword of the Spirit is the word of God, the Christian's only offensive weapon to use in his fight against sin and error. Knowledge of the word enables one to use the sword effectively. The one who does not know the word cannot wage successful warfare against the devil.

7. "Prayer." Prayer also protects against the Devil's attacks. Prayer is part of the Christian's protective armor.

Are you prepared for the battle?

The Danger of Entanglement

Paul warned of the danger of a soldier becoming so entangled in the affairs of this life that he does not do the work of a soldier. He wrote, "Thou therefore endure hardness, as a good soldier of Jesus Christ. No man that warreth entangleth himself with the affairs of this life; that he may please him who had chosen him to be a soldier" (2 Tim. 2:3,4).

Far too many twentieth century Christians have forgotten that a war in is progress. They are like the watchmaker who enlisted in the army and began to repair watches on the side. As more and more soldiers became aware that he could repair watches, his "business" grew. One day the commander called the army to battle. When the watchmaker did not answer the roll call, the commander came looking for him and found him in his tent repairing watches. The commander said, "Come on, we're ready for battle." The watchmaker replied, "I can't go right now; I have to finish fixing this watch." The watchmaker had forgotten why he had enlisted in the army. Similarly, too many Christians have forgotten why they enlisted as soldiers in the army of Christ. They have become too involved in bowling, lakeside cottages, television, baseball, etc. that they have little time left for Christ. A good soldier will not form alliances that hamper his service in the army.

Ready to Suffer

The good soldier must be ready to "endure hardness" (2 Tim. 2:3). Soldiers know that they sometimes have to endure hardships. They are able to get by on rations, to go without a mattress and box springs, to forego television, to know that they are being shot at, etc. They know that service in the army might bring bodily injury or even death. Nevertheless, they are willing to suffer hardship as soldiers.

Similarly, some Christians have been called upon to suffer death as a soldier of Christ (cf. 2 Tim. 4:6-8). Many have endured ostracism, mockery, and other forms of social persecution for Christ (2 Tim. 3:12). That comes with being a soldier. We need to be prepared to suffer as a soldier.

The Assurance of Victory

Unlike other wars, the outcome of this one was settled long before it ever began. Jesus Christ will conquer. We do not have to worry about what will happen to us in the event that Satan wins the war. John saw the victory and wrote:

> And I saw an angel standing in the sun; and he cried with a loud voice, saying to all the fowls that fly in the midst of heaven, Come and gather yourselves together unto the supper of the great God; that ye may eat the flesh of kings, and the flesh of the captains, and the flesh of mighty men, and the flesh of horses, and of them that sit on them, and the flesh of all men, both free and bond, both small and great. And I saw the beast, and the kings of the earth, and their armies, gathered together to make war against him that sat on the horse, and against his army. And the beast was taken, and with him the false prophet that wrought miracles before him, with which he deceived them that had received the mark of the beast, and them that worshipped his image. These both were cast alive into a lake of fire burning with brimstone (Rev. 19:17-20).

The final outcome of this spiritual conflict has been forever settled. We who fight for Jesus will be the victors. We shall overcome; victory is assured!

Conclusion

When Paul's death was visibly imminent, he wrote, "For I am now ready to be offered, and the time of my departure is at hand. I have fought a good fight, I have finished my course, I have kept the faith: henceforth there is laid up for me a crown of righteousness, which the Lord the righteous judge, shall give me at that day: and not to be only, but unto all them also that love his appearing" (2 Tim. 4:6-8). Can you say with Paul, "I have fought a good fight"? Or, have you become so involved in the entangling affairs of this life that you have forgotten the battle? Are you watching while others do the fighting, suffer the injuries, and even die for Christ? Are you a spiritual pacifist? Christ has enrolled you in his army. The battle is in full array. Take up your armor and fight!

Questions
Matching
____ 1. Fight the good fight.   a.   2 Tim. 4:7
____ 2. War a good warfare.   b.   1 Tim. 6:12
____ 3. Endure hardness as a good soldier.   c.   Phile. 2
____ 4. I have fought a good fight.   d.   2 Tim. 2:3
____ 5. Fellow soldier.   e.   1 Tim. 1:18

True or False
____ 1. Some Christians are exempt from service in Christ's army.
____ 2. The devil is presently assaulting Christians.
____ 3. The church should use weapons such as newspaper articles, TV programs, radio programs, and other means to oppose the devil.
____ 4. The Christian can oppose Satan's army by such weapons as guns, gossip, and slander.
____ 5. A soldier of Christ should not condemn other religions.

Short Answer
1. What significant differences are there between physical and spiritual warfare (Eph. 6:12; Jn. 18:36)? _____
    _____

2. Name some carnal weapons which cannot be used in the battle against Satan (2 Cor. 10:3-4). _____
    _____

3. What weapons may be used and how are they described (2 Cor. 10:3-4)?
    _____
    _____

4. What obligation does a Christian have to oppose false teaching and false teachers (Tit. 1:11; 1 Tim. 5:20; Eph. 5:11)? _____
    _____

5. How might one undermine the work of opposing false doctrine and false teachers? _____

6. The Christian armor (Eph. 6:11-18):
    a.   What is "truth" in 6:14? _____
         How is this essential to staying faithful? _____
         _____

    b.   What is "righteousness"? _____
         How is this essential to staying faithful? _____
         _____

    c.   What are "feet shod with the preparation of the gospel"? _____
         _____
         How are they essential to staying faithful? _____
         _____

d. What is "faith"? _____
    How is it essential to staying faithful? _____
    _____

e. What is the "helmet of salvation"? _____
    How is it essential to staying faithful? _____
    _____

f. What is the "sword of the Spirit"? _____
    How is it essential to staying faithful? _____
    _____

g. How can a person become effective in using it? _____
    _____

7. What things tend to entangle Christians so that they cannot do the work of a soldier (2 Tim. 2:3-4)? _____
    _____

8. What have you suffered as a soldier in Christ's army (2 Tim. 2:3-4; 3:12)?
    _____
    _____

9. What does Revelation 19:17-20 guarantee about the outcome of this battle? _____
    _____

10. What should I do today to guarantee that I can say, as did Paul, "I have fought a good fight"? _____
    _____

11. List some spiritual songs that emphasize that we are soldiers of Christ.
    _____
    _____
    _____
    _____

Lesson 9

A Christian Is . . . A Priest

The apostle Peter wrote, "Ye also, as lively stones, are built up a spiritual house, *an holy priesthood, to offer up spiritual sacrifices*, acceptable to God by Jesus Christ. . . . But ye are a chosen generation, *a royal priesthood*, a peculiar people; that ye should shew forth the praises of him who hath called you out of darkness into his marvellous light" (1 Pet. 2:5, 9). In these two verses, Peter described the Christian as a priest. Thus, in our consideration of what a Christian is, we need to consider the significance of being designated a priest.

The Concept of Priesthood

The Old Testament describes a priest for us. A priest is one who is duly authorized to minister in sacred things, particularly to offer sacrifices at the altar and who acts as mediator between God and man (Heb. 5:1). In the Patriarchal age, we are introduced to priests such as Melchizedek (Gen. 14:18-24), Moses' father-in-law, Jethro (Exod. 3:1), and many pagan priests. In the Mosaical age, the Lord designated the descendants of Aaron as the priestly family (Exod. 29; Lev. 8). Through a ceremony of consecration, the descendants of Aaron were set apart to serve as a priest. Once appointed, the priest could offer animal sacrifice, offer burnt incense, light the lamp in the tabernacle, and teach the law of God to the people.

When Christ came, he changed the priesthood. Jesus serves as a priest after the order of Melchizedek (Heb. 3:1; 5:10; 7), rather than as a priest of the tribe of Levi. His office is not based on genealogical descent (Heb. 7:16). He did not take this office upon himself; rather, he was chosen of God (Heb. 5:4-6). He has an unchangeable priesthood which continues forever (Heb. 7:24-28). Inasmuch as Jesus is our high priest, the law had to change (Heb. 7:12,18). The law of Moses was annulled in order that the law of Christ, with the priesthood of Jesus might be established. In the law of Christ, there is no evidence of a separate priesthood, such as existed in the Levitical priesthood of the law of Moses.

The Influence of Catholicism

Catholicism established a priesthood similar to that of the law of Moses, different in that it is not based on genealogical descent through the tribe of Levi. Catholicism has influenced the thinking of most people with reference to the concept of priests. In the Catholic Church, a separate group of people are designated priests (a clergy). These men have a special function, special qualifications, and special privileges. They constitute a separate group of people (clergy) from the rest of the people (laity). The Catholic concept has also been adopted by some Protestant churches.

In Catholic thought, the Lord transferred to the Apostles special powers which have been handed down in an unbroken chain to the church today. These powers are not to be confused with the ability to work miracles to confirm the revelation given by the Holy Spirit through them, which miracles ceased when the New Testament revelation was confirmed. Rather, the special authority and powers which the Apostles are thought to have received and which are then passed down from one generation to another by a special ceremony of laying on of hands include the following: (a) the right to offer Mass or the Eucharist (the Catholic concept of the mass is the continual sacrificing of the literal body and blood of Jesus) ; (b) the right to administer baptism; (c) the right to absolve sin (consequently, a Catholic must confess his sins to a priest who pronounces him forgiven). Only a specially ordained priest can perform any of these acts. Unless a person has been ordained as a priest, he cannot perform these acts.

The Catholic concept of the priesthood places the church, through its priests, as a mediator between man and God. The Lord Jesus Christ is the one mediator between God and man (1 Tim. 2:5). The *International Standard Bible Encyclopedia* summarizes this point very well:

> In ancient times it was held that men in general could not have direct access to God, that any approach to Him must be mediated by some member of the class of priests, who alone could approach God, and who must accordingly be employed by other men to represent them before Him. This whole conception vanishes in the light of Christianity. By virtue of their relation to Christ all believers have direct approach to God, and consequently, as this right of approach was formerly a priestly privilege, priesthood may now be predicated of every Christian (Vol. IV, p. 2446).

There is no special class of "clergy" which serves as a mediator between Jesus and man. Rather, one approaches the Father through the mediatorship of Jesus Christ. This was one of the basic tenets of truth re-discovered during the Protestant Reformation and generally designated "the priesthood of all believers." The principle asserts that every individual has direct access to God through Jesus Christ and, therefore, does not need to approach God through a priest.

The Priesthood of All Believers

Recognizing that every Christian is a priest, we now look for the pertinent points of emphasis in stating that the Christian is a priest. Here are some points:

1. The priest must be consecrated. Even as the priest was set apart as holy unto God (Exod. 29), so also must a person be set apart to serve as God's priests today. A man is sanctified, set apart, when he obeys the gospel in baptism (1 Cor. 6:11). At that point he may be designated as "holy unto the Lord" (cf. Exod. 28:36; 1 Pet. 1:15).

2. The priest must be pure. A man could not serve as a priest if he was declared unclean (Lev. 22:1-16). There were a number of things which might make a man unclean under the law of Moses, including contact with the dead, unclean animals, and lepers. In the priesthood of Christ, sin defiles the man (Matt. 15:17-20). Hence, a Christian must avoid the defilements of sin in order to serve as a priest. One who walks after the flesh (Gal. 5:19-21) cannot offer spiritual worship to God; he must put away his wickedness and seek the Lord's forgiveness before he is qualified to offer worship to God.

3. The priest offers sacrifices to the Lord. The Levitical priest served at the altar of burnt offering and incense. In the New Testament era, the sacrifice for sin was offered once for all, Jesus Christ offering himself as a once-for-all sacrifice for sin (Heb. 9:14, 24-28; 10:4,10-14). Nevertheless, the Christian can offer spiritual sacrifices (1 Pet. 2:5) of worship to God. We do not serve at a literal altar, offering incense and animal sacrifice. We do not offer sacrifices to atone for sin since the blood of Jesus was shed once for all time to atone for sin. The Christian, who is a priest, offers spiritual worship of the following kinds:

a. His body as a living sacrifice. Paul wrote, "I beseech you therefore, brethren, by the mercies of God, that ye present your bodies a living sacrifice, holy, acceptable to God, which is your reasonable service" (Rom. 12:1; cf. 2 Cor. 8:5; Gal. 2:20; Phil. 1:20-21). In contrast to a dead animal sacrifice which was slaughtered and burned one time on an altar, the Christian brings his body as a living sacrifice to God, his whole life being dedicated to the Lord's service.

b. His speech, the fruit of his lips. "By him therefore let us offer the sacrifice of praise to God continually, that is, the fruit of our lips giving thanks to his name" (Heb. 13:15). Our prayers ascend to God as the smoke of the incense altar (Rev. 8:3-4). Our songs offer praise to him and petition him for blessings. The Christian's tongue can be used to preach his gospel. This is the sacrifice of the fruit of our lips.

 c. His good works of benevolence are sacrifices well pleasing to God. Continuing in Hebrews, the writer exhorts, "But to do good and to communicate forget not: for with such sacrifices God is well pleased" (Heb. 13:16). When Paul brought the contribution from the Gentile Christians to the poor saints at Jerusalem, he designated these alms as "offerings" (Acts 24:17). We offer sacrifices unto God when we follow the example of the Good Samaritan (Lk. 10:25-37), doing good to all men but especially to the household of faith (Gal. 6:10).

 d. His support of gospel preachers. When Paul described the contribution that the church at Philippi had sent to him, he described it as an offering. He wrote, "But I have all, and abound: I am full, having received of Epaphroditus the things which were sent from you, an odour of a sweet smell, a sacrifice acceptable, wellpleasing to God" (Phil. 4:18). When a Christian makes a contribution on the first day of the week (1 Cor. 16:1-2) to be used in supporting gospel preachers and relieving the needs of the poor among the saints, he makes a sacrifice to God.

 e. His life. For Paul, serving Christ resulted in his death at the hand of the Roman government. As he described his death, he pictured it as a sacrifice offered to God. "For I am now ready to be *offered*, and the time of my departure is at hand. I have fought a good fight, I have finished my course, I have kept the faith: henceforth there is laid up for me a crown of righteousness, which the Lord, the righteous judge, shall give me at that day: and not to me only, but unto all them also that love his appearing" (2 Tim. 4:6-8). In Revelation 6, John saw the souls of those having been slain for the word of God "under the altar" (6:9), as a sacrifice to God.

 These are sacrifices of worship which every Christian can offer to God.

 4. A priest must teach the Lord's word. In giving his charge to Aaron, the Lord commanded that he "teach the children of Israel all the statutes which the Lord hath spoken unto them" (Lev. 10:11). As the Lord's priest, every Christian needs to be teaching the Lord's word as he has opportunity.

Conclusion
 In the days of the judges, Eli's sons interfered with the Lord's worship because of their ungodliness (1 Sam. 2:12, 17, 22). The people resented bringing worship to God because of the sins that they saw in the priests. When people consider you as the Lord's priests, how do they perceive the Lord's worship? What kind of priest are you?

Questions
Multiple Choice
____ 1. During the patriarchal age, the Old Testament describes (a) Moses, (b) Noah, (c) Melchizedek as a priest of God.

____ 2. Under the law of Moses, a priest had to be a descendant of the tribe of (a) Judah, (b) Levi, (c) David.

____ 3. Jesus could not serve as a priest under the law of Moses because he descended from the tribe of (a) Judah, (b) Levi, (c) Benjamin.

____ 4. Jesus' priesthood is (a) not based on genealogical descent, (b) an everlasting priesthood, (c) proof that the law has changed, (d) all of the above, (e) none of the above.

____ 5. A separate priesthood is part of the law of (a) Moses, (b) Christ.

True or False
____ 1. Catholicism established a separate priesthood similar to the Levitical priesthood.

____ 2. The priest in the Catholic Church has the same role as the New Testament preacher.

____ 3. According to Catholic doctrine, in celebrating the mass, the Catholic priest offers the literal body and blood of Jesus as a sacrifice for sin.

____ 4. As a representative of the Catholic Church, the priest has the right to absolve from sin.

____ 5. When a Christian makes a public confession of sin, the preacher grants forgiveness of sin to him.

____ 6. Confession to one another is just as effectual as confession to a priest, according to Catholic doctrine.

____ 7. The priesthood concept created a clergy-laity distinction.

Short Answer
1. What is the work of a priest (Heb. 5:1)? _____
   _____

2. When does a Christian become a priest (1 Cor. 6:11)? _____
   _____

3. What caused a Levitical priest to be unclean (Lev. 22:1-16)?_____
   _____

4. What causes a Christian to be impure (Matt. 15:17-20)? _____
   _____

5. What is the atoning sacrifice for sins today (Heb. 9:14, 24-28; 10:4, 10-14)? _____
   _____

6. In what sense can a Christian offer sacrifice (1 Pet. 2:5)?_____
   _____

7. How does one offer his body as a living sacrifice to God (Rom. 12:1; cf. 2

Cor. 8:5; Gal. 2:20; Phil. 1:20-21)? _____

_____

8. What makes this sacrifice superior to an animal sacrifice? _____

_____

9. How may one offer the "fruit of his lips" as a sacrifice to God (Heb. 13:15)? _____

_____

10. How would this understanding affect our singing? _____

_____

11. How may one present his money as a sacrifice to the Lord (Heb. 13:16; Acts 24:17; 1 Cor. 16:1-2)? _____

_____

12. How did Paul view his death at the hands of the Roman government (2 Tim. 4:6-8)? _____

_____

13. What impact does an ungodly Christian have on worship to God (cf. 1 Sam. 2:12, 17, 22)? _____

_____

14. What attitude did God have toward a worshiper who brought the left-overs to sacrifice to God (Mal. 1:6-11)? _____

_____

Lesson 10

A Christian Is . . . Called of God

The New Testament refers to God's people as the "called of God" in such passages as the following:

> Jude, the servant of Jesus Christ, and brother of James, to them that are . . . called (Jude 1).

> But we preach Christ crucified, unto the Jews a stumblingblock, and unto the Greeks foolishness; but unto them which are called, both Jews and Greeks, Christ the power of God, and the wisdom of God (1 Cor. 1:23-24).

> Among whom are ye also the called of Jesus Christ (Rom. 1:6).

In learning what a Christian is through the study of the terms by which he is described, we must include a study of him being designated the "called" of God.

Definition of the Term

The term translated "called" (*kletos*) comes from the verb "to call" (*kaleo*). It is the verb from which the word church (*ekklesia*) is also derived. The verb "to call" is sometimes used in the sense of "to invite." Because it is used for God's invitation through the preaching of the gospel, the word takes on a technical sense to mean those who have accepted God's invitation which was addressed to them in the gospel. The church is composed of "the called out ones" and saints are "the called" of God.

In the parable of the wedding feast (Matt. 22:1-14), Jesus compared God's work of redemption to a wedding feast. In the wedding feast, the king prepared a great feast for the marriage of his son. Then he sent forth his servants to call them who had been invited to the feast. In the parable those who had been invited made light of the feast and did not come. Because of the disdainful manner in which the invited guests treated the invitation, the king turned to the highways and byways to invite whosoever will to come to the feast. The application of the parable was to the kingdom of God. The Lord made preparations for the coming of the kingdom, announcing before-hand to the Jewish nation that the kingdom was to be established. When the Messiah came, they treated him disdainfully. Consequently, the Lord turned to the Gentiles inviting whosoever will to come to the kingdom. Those who came were those "called" to the wedding feast.

Men value invitations on the basis of who extended the invitation (e.g. an invitation from the President of the United States is more valuable than an invitation to join me at a fast food restaurant). Because of this, our invitation to participate in the Lord's kingdom should be cherished above all invitations. Our invitation to be a part of the kingdom of God comes from God himself (Eph. 1:18; Phil. 3:14; 2 Tim. 1:9). God has invited us to the benefits which this calling brings, not on the basis of our good works, but on the basis of his grace (2 Tim. 1:9). We do not deserve the salvation which he has invited us to enjoy. Access to this salvation has been made possible for us through Jesus (Gal. 1:6 – called into the grace of Christ).

We should treasure our blessing to be one of those "called" (invited) by God to the blessings of the gospel.

To What We Are Called

When men are given an invitation, they want to know to what they have been invited. Here are the characteristics of our calling:

1. To repentance. Jesus said, "I am not come to call the righteous, but sinners to repentance" (Matt. 9:13).

2. To fellowship with Christ. "God is faithful, by whom ye were called unto the fellowship of his Son Jesus Christ our Lord" (1 Cor. 1:9).

3. To peace. (a) With God – "God hath called us to peace" (1 Cor. 7:15); Jesus "came and preached peace" (Eph. 2:17) – reconciliation with God through the blood of Jesus. (b) With oneself – the gospel of Christ gives one a "peace that passeth all understanding" (Phil. 4:7). (c) With others – the Christian is to allow the "peace of God" to "rule in your hearts" (Col. 3:14-15), making every effort to be at peace with his fellowman (Rom. 12:18).

4. To eternal life. "Fight the good fight of faith, lay hold on eternal life, whereunto thou art also called" (1 Tim. 6:12). Because we are invited to receive eternal life, we are "called" to "inherit a blessing" (1 Pet. 3:9) and "unto eternal glory" (1 Pet. 5:10).

5. To citizenship in God's kingdom. "That ye would walk worthy of God, who hath called you unto his kingdom and glory" (1 Thess. 2:12).

6. To liberty. "For brethren, ye have been called unto liberty" (Gal. 5:13). The freedom to which we have been called is freedom from sin's guilt and damnation (Jn. 8:32).

The Nature of the Calling

Because the calling originates from God and consummates in our inheritance of heaven, it is called a "high calling" (Phil. 3:14), a holy calling (2 Tim. 1:9), a heavenly calling (Heb. 3:1) and a calling with hope (Eph. 1:18; 4:4). Christians value the calling from God just as highly as did the apostles who so described their invitation to salvation.

The Method of Calling

How does God call us? There have been a number of explanations of how men are called by God. Calvinism believes that God has predestinated all men into two classes: the elect and reprobate. Those whom God chooses to save (elect) are given an irresistible, miraculous call of grace. Before men are received into the fellowship of the church, they have to give their testimony of how God called them and be voted into the church by its members. Subjective experiences are the evidence that one has been called by God. Even today, men testify of God speaking directly to them in some "still, small voice," giving them a tongue-speaking experience, or some other outward sign that they have been called.

While Jesus was on earth, he called men directly to be his disciples. When Jesus wanted Peter, Andrew, James and John to be his disciples, he went to where they were working and called them to be his disciples, saying, "Come, follow me" (Matt. 4:18-22). These men were then taught by Jesus.

While on earth, Jesus said that coming to God requires that one be taught the gospel. In other words, Jesus used words to call men to be his disciples.

> No man can come to me, except the Father which hath sent me draw him: and I will raise him up at the last day. It is written in the prophets, And they shall be all taught of God. Every man that hath heard, and hath learned of the Father, cometh unto me (Jn. 6:44-45).

After Jesus ascended to the Father, men are still called to be his disciples through being taught of God – hearing, learning, and coming. That occurs through the preaching of the gospel. Hence, Paul wrote that God has "called you by our gospel" (2 Thess. 2:14).

The great invitations of the gospel are extended through preaching. Jesus invited men burdened with the guilt of their sin saying, "Come unto me, all ye that labour and are heavy laden, and I will give you rest. Take my yoke upon you, and learn of me; for I am meek and lowly in heart: and ye shall find rest unto your souls. For my yoke is easy, and my burden is light" (Matt. 11:28-30). John described the Lord's invitation saying, "Behold, I stand at the door, and knock: if any man hear my voice, and open the door, I will come in to him, and will sup with him, and he with me" (Rev. 3:20). Again, "And the Spirit and the bride say, Come. And let him that heareth say, Come. And let him that is athirst come. And whosoever will, let him take the water of life freely" (Rev. 22:17).

Our songs emphasize the calling of God through the gospel. One says that God is "calling yet." "Shall I not rise? Can I His loving voice despise, And basely his kind care repay? He calls me still; can I delay?" ("God Calling Yet") Another says, "Jesus is tenderly calling thee home – calling today, calling today" ("Jesus Is Calling"). Another said, "I can hear by Savior calling" ("Where He Leads Me") and expresses the resolution to follow him saying, "Where he leads me I will follow." Can you hear the Lord calling you through his gospel?

The Corinthians: An Example

We can see how men are called of God by looking at the Corinthians. They are described as the "called" of God (1 Cor. 1:24). How were they called? The book of Acts tells us that Paul preached at Corinth and "many of the Corinthians hearing believed, and were baptized" (Acts 18:8).

The High Calling Demands High Living

The apostle Paul exhorted, "I therefore, the prisoner of the Lord, beseech you that ye walk worthy of the vocation wherewith ye are called" (Eph. 4:1). The heavenly calling requires godly living. In the parable of the wedding feast, one came to the feast without a "wedding garment." The Lord bound him hand and foot and cast him into outer darkness saying, "Many are called, but few are chosen" (Matt. 22:11-14).

We understand the need to show respect for the occasion of our invitation in social events. If I were to receive an invitation to a celebration at the White House, I would not show up in blue jeans and a T-shirt. To so dress would be to show disrespect for the occasion and him who invited me.

For a man who has received a heavenly calling not to show respect for the nature of that call is demeaning to God. We show respect, not merely by the clothes we wear to worship, but by the character we have. God has called us out of darkness into his marvelous light (1 Pet. 2:9); "for God hath not called us unto uncleanness, but unto holiness. He therefore that despiseth, despiseth not man, but God, who hath also given unto us his holy Spirit" (1 Thess. 4:7-8). To show respect for the calling, I need to be dressed in the robes of righteousness that the beauty of holiness might be seen in me.

Conclusion

We are privileged to have received the heavenly calling. What a blessed people we are to have been called of God into the fellowship of him and his Son throughout the endless ages to share heaven with them. Let us walk worthily of that great calling.

Short Answer Questions

1. List at least three passages which describe Christians as the "called." __

    _____

2. From the parable of the wedding feast (Matt. 22:1-14), answer these questions:

    a. Who is represented by the king? _____

    b. Who is represented by the son? _____

    c. What is represented by the wedding feast? _____

    d. Who are represented by those who treated the invitation disdainfully? _____

    e. Who are represented by those who were in the highways and byways? _____

    f. Who is represented by the one who did not have on a wedding garment? _____

3. Who has called man (Eph. 1:18; Phil. 3:14; 2 Tim. 1:9)? _____

4. Why is our calling described as a call to repentance (Matt. 9:13)? _____

    _____

5. Why is being called to the fellowship of Jesus a treasured invitation (1 Cor. 1:9)? _____

    _____

6. To what kinds of peace have we been called (Eph. 2:17; Phil. 4:7; Rom. 12:18)? _____

    _____

    _____

7. What blessing is described as part of our calling in 1 Timothy 6:12; 1 Peter 3:9; 5:10? _____

8. To what kind of liberty have we been called (Gal. 5:13)?_____

    _____

9. How do these verses describe our calling?

    a. Eph. 1:18; 4:4 – _____

    b. Phil. 3:14 – _____

    c. 2 Tim. 1:9 – _____

    d. Heb. 3:1 – _____

10. How did Jesus "call" the apostles (Matt. 4:18-22)? _____

    _____

11. How does John 6:44-45 show men are able to come to God? _____

    _____

    _____

12. How does 2 Thessalonians 2:14 say men are called by God? _____

    _____

13. List some of Jesus' invitations to men to be saved. _____

    _____

14. How did the "called" Corinthians (1 Cor. 1:24) receive their calling (Acts 18:8)? _____

_____

15. What kind of living does our calling demand (Eph. 4:1)? _____

_____

16. What kinds of conduct do not fit our calling? _____

_____

17. How does ungodly living show disrespect for God who called us? _____

_____

Lesson 11

A Christian Is . . . A Worker

The Lord described Christians as "workers" and "laborers" (cf. 2 Tim. 2:15; 2 Cor. 6:1; Phil. 4:3). This figure of speech reveals something about what being a Christian means. Let us study what this term reveals about being a Christian.

Laborers in the Vineyard

In Matthew 20, the Lord gave the parable of the laborers in the vineyard. He said, "For the kingdom of heaven is like unto a man that is an householder, which went out early in the morning to hire labourers into his vineyard" (20:1). The parable relates how the Lord's grace was shown to those hired later in the day to make them equal in reward with those who worked through the heat of the day. However, the parable also emphasizes that Christians in the Lord's church are compared to laborers in a vineyard. There is work to do and we are to be the workers.

Christians are the workers who do the work of the Lord. We have been created for good works (Eph. 2:10). Jesus redeemed us that we might be a people "zealous of good works" (Tit. 2:14), "ready to every good work" (Tit. 3:1), and "careful to maintain good works" (Tit. 3:8). Dorcas was a model Christian inasmuch as she was "full of good works" (Acts 9:36; cf. 1 Tim. 5:10 for good works women can do).

We should be "abounding" in good works (1 Cor. 15:58). As a child, I remember hearing a discussion on the subject, "What is the least percentage that a Christian can give to the Lord and still go to heaven?" That question reflects an attitude toward all of the Lord's service. Men ask, "Do I have to attend all of the services in order to go to heaven?" Such questions display an attitude of "least-possible-service" which is undermining the Lord's work in many congregations. Instead of asking, "What is the least that I can do and still go to heaven?" we should be trying to see what is the most that we can do in the Lord's kingdom. Notice these passages:

Therefore, my beloved brethren, be ye stedfast, unmoveable, always abounding in the work of the Lord, forasmuch as ye know that your labour is not in vain in the Lord (1 Cor. 15:58).

Charge them . . . that they do good, that they be rich in good works, ready to distribute, willing to communicate (1 Tim. 6:17-18).

That ye might walk worthy of the Lord unto all pleasing, being fruitful in every good work, and increasing in the knowledge of God (Col. 1:10).

There can be no doubt that the Christian is to be busy in the work of the Lord.

Far too often, Christians view the time they spend in attending the worship services as the only work they are expected to do. For this reason, Jehovah's Witnesses describe most church members as "pew-sitters" and "bench-warmers." The assembling with the saints to worship should not be viewed as doing the work of the Lord. Rather, we should assemble to learn enough and be sufficiently encouraged to go out to do the work of the Lord. When we come together, we should hear lessons designed to encourage us to "go into all the world and preach the gospel," to "visit the fatherless and widows in their affliction," to "bring up our children in the nurture and admonition of the Lord," etc. Then, we should leave the building determined to do these works. The assembly is designed to provoke one another to do good works (Heb. 10:24-25); assemblying is not the work itself!

Workers Together

The Scriptures also emphasize that Christians are "fellow workers" (Rom. 16:21). In 1 Corinthians 3, Paul emphasized that Christians work together in the Lord's kingdom. In emphasizing the unity of the church to a divided congregation (some were saying, "I of Paul, I of Apollos, and I of Cephas" – 1:10-13), Paul stressed that these men were working together. He said, "I have planted, Apollos watered. . . . Now he that planteth and he that watereth are one" (1 Cor. 3:6,8). These verses emphasize that Christians should work together.

In 1 Corinthians 12, Paul compared the church to a body, the individual members being compared to a hand, foot, ear, and eye. The body needs what each member contributes; each member contributes something different from every other member. In the Lord's kingdom, we Christians should recognize that each of us is different and can contribute something different to the Lord's work. One man can preach, another can lead singing, another can teach a children's class, another can clean the building, another can influence people to attend worship with him. There is no competition or spirit of rivalry among the members. We are all working together to accomplish the Lord's work. A warm spirit of cooperation should exist among the members of a local congregation as we put our hands and hearts together in the Lord's work. Bickering, backbiting, fussing and fighting interfere with the Lord's work and should not be tolerated in a congregation.

Workers Together With God

Paul also added, "For we are labourers together with God" (1 Cor. 3:9). We work in the kingdom; we work together with others in the kingdom; we work together with other Christians and *with the Lord*. If a man were privileged to join hands with the President to accomplish some important work, he would think himself honored. How much more should he feel honored to be able to join hands with the Lord to accomplish the most important work in the world!

We have the privilege of working with God to accomplish the salvation of souls. God has provided the sacrifice, the gift of his Son, that men may be saved. He has revealed the gospel of salvation to us in the New Testament (Rom. 1:16). We have the privilege and responsibility to take this saving gospel to all of mankind (Matt. 28:18-20; 2 Tim. 2:2). When a Christian teaches his friend the gospel and that friend obeys the gospel, he has worked with God in saving that man's immortal soul. What a privilege to join hands with God in saving another's soul!

A Workman That Needeth Not To Be Ashamed

Paul exhorted us to be diligent in the work of the Lord when he wrote, "Study to shew thyself approved unto God, a workman that needeth not to be ashamed, rightly dividing the word of truth" (2 Tim. 2:15). By hard work, Christians can be workers who have no reason to be ashamed when God calls them for judgment. The figure of speech used here pictures a worker, who has been assigned a job by his boss, having his work examined. If he has worked hard and done his job well, he has no reason to be ashamed. If he has been lazy and done sloppy work, he will be ashamed when his boss checks his work.

The implication of the text is that those workers in the Lord's vineyard who are not diligent in their work will have reason to be ashamed. The Scriptures warn of the sin of knowing to do good and not doing it (Jas. 4:17; Lk. 12:47). The parables of the virgins (Matt. 25:1-13), the talents (Matt. 25:14-30), and the separation of the sheep and goats (Matt. 25:31-46) emphasize the importance of being busy doing the works the Lord commanded us to do; in these parables, those who did not do the works of the Lord were lost.

The sin of negligence in the Lord's work is destroying congregations. Long ago, the wise man observed a physical truth which is also true spiritually, "He also that is slothful in his work is brother to him that is a great waster" (Prov. 18:19). Solomon knew that one does not have to tear down a house to destroy it; all that he must do is fail to maintain it. A person does not have to burn a field to destroy a crop; all that he needs to do is to fail to cultivate and weed it. Similarly, the Lord's house, the church, can be destroyed by negligence and slothfulness. A church can be destroyed by laziness in the Lord's work. If we do not convert more people than we lose through moving, apostasy, and death, the church will eventually dwindle away to nothing. Surely we can see our need for zeal in the Lord's work.

What Can I Do?

Sometimes people are motivated to be busy in the Lord's work, but lack direction. They ask, "What can I do?" Here is a list of things that Christians can do. Check off the ones that you can and are willing to do:

Job	Can	Will
Worship Services:		
Lead singing	____	____
Lead prayer	____	____
Teach a Bible class	____	____
Serve Lord's supper	____	____
Preach	____	____
Make Announcements	____	____
Miscellaneous jobs		
Prepare schedule for worship	____	____
Be Treasurer	____	____
Clean building	____	____
Repairs on building	____	____
Clean baptistry	____	____
Painting	____	____
Maintain the grounds (flower beds, etc.)	____	____
Work on bulletin	____	____
Prepare meeting cards	____	____
Work among members		
Visit the sick	____	____
Visit the shut-ins	____	____
Invite visitors for a meal	____	____
Invite new members for a meal	____	____
Plan a get-together for congregation	____	____
Plan a get-together for young people	____	____
Visit those who miss worship	____	____
Provide transportation to those who need it	____	____
Evangelism		
Organize a home Bible study	____	____
Invite someone to worship	____	____
Give someone a tract	____	____
Talk to someone about Jesus	____	____
Encourage those we support	____	____

Try to restore someone who has fallen away	____	____
Edification		
Visit an area meeting	____	____
Read your Bible daily	____	____
Pray regularly	____	____
Prepare for Bible class	____	____
Be sure your children are prepared for class	____	____

Sometimes, members criticize a congregation saying, "They are not doing anything at this congregation." "They" includes each of us. I should ask myself, "Am I doing anything?"

Our songs remind us of our work in the Lord's kingdom. "O, the things we may do, you and I; O, the love we can give if we try." "There is room in the kingdom of God, my brother, for the small things that you can do." "There is much to do, there's work on every hand, Hark! the cry for help comes ringing thru the land; Jesus calls for reapers, I must active be, What wilt thou, O Master? Here am I, send me." "I want to be a worker for the Lord, I want to love and trust his holy word; I want to sing and pray, and be busy every day In the kingdom of the Lord."

Conclusion

A Christian is a worker or laborer in the vineyard of the Lord. Are you a worker? Are you ashamed of the work you have done for the Lord? The Bible says, "They were judged every man, according to their works" (Rev. 20:12). Jesus warned, "Behold, I come quickly; and my reward is with me, to give every man according as his work shall be" (Rev. 22:12). "Wherefore, my beloved, as ye have always obeyed, not as in my presence only, but now much more in my absence, work out your own salvation with fear and trembling" (Phil. 2:12).

Jesus emphasized that our good works cause others to be attracted to the light of the gospel. He said, "Let your light so shine before men, that they may see your good works, and glorify your Father which is in heaven" (Matt. 5:16). What do your friends and neighbors see when they look at you?

Questions
Matching

____ 1. Created for good works		a.	Acts 9:36
____ 2. A worker that needs not be ashamed		b.	1 Cor. 15:58
____ 3. Full of good works		c.	2 Tim. 2:15
____ 4. Zealous of good works		d.	Tit. 3:8
____ 5. Careful to maintain good works		e.	Eph. 2:10
____ 6. Abounding in the work of the Lord		f.	Tit. 2:14

Short Answer

1. What disposition toward the Lord's work should characterize the Christian (1 Cor. 15:58; Tit. 2:14)? _____

2. What is wrong with the attitude manifested by such questions as, "Do I have to attend all the worship services?" _____

3. Are Christians with this attitude usually "busy" doing the Lord's work? _____

4. Is the worship assembly the "work" which we do for the Lord? _____

5. What is the purpose of the worship assembly according to Hebrews 10:24-25? _____

6. What relationship should exist among Christian workers (1 Cor. 3:6, 8)? _____

7. How do our individual abilities contribute to the overall function of the body (1 Cor. 12:12-31)? _____

8. How can Christians work "with God" (1 Cor. 3:9)? _____

9. What might cause a Christian to be a worker that is ashamed (2 Tim. 2:15)? _____

10. What is said of the one who fails to do what he should in these passages:
    a. James 4:17 – _____
    b. Matt. 25:14-30 – _____
    c. Matt. 25:31-46 – _____

11. In what way is a lazy person like a destroyer (Prov. 18:19)?_____

12. On what basis will men be judged (Rev. 20:12-22; 22:12)? _____

13. What impact do our good works have on evangelism (Matt. 5:16)?_____
    _____

Lesson 12

A Christian Is . . . A Member of the Body

The Lord used the comparison of the Christian to a member of a body on several occasions (1 Cor. 12:12-31; Rom. 12:4-8). Even as we can learn what being a Christian means by studying how he is a soldier of Christ, a priest, and a saint, we can also learn what a Christian is by understanding how he is a member of the body of Christ.

Many Members, But One Body

Paul wrote, "For as the body is one, and hath many members, and all the members of that one body, being many, are one body: so also is Christ" (1 Cor. 12:12). Again Paul said, "There is one body" (Eph. 4:4). The oneness of the church is emphasized by the figure of the church as the body of Christ. The concept of modern denominationalism – many different bodies – is contrary to the concept of the church as the body of Christ.

Reconciliation to God occurs in the one body. Paul wrote, "And that he might reconcile both (Jew and Gentile, mw) unto God in one body by the cross" (Eph. 2:16). If one is reconciled to God, he will be reconciled in the one body, the Lord's church. There is no reconciliation outside that one body. The person who is not a member of the Lord's church has not been reconciled to God. Jesus is "the saviour of the body" (Eph. 5:23). If a person is not a member of that body, he will not be saved by Jesus.

Some have the concept that many different bodies are necessary because men are different. Men have always been different. The Jews were different from the Gentiles in the apostolic age when Paul wrote, "And that he might reconcile both (Jew and Gentile, mw) unto God in one body by the cross" (Eph. 2:16). If there ever had been justification for two bodies in which different groups could be reconciled to God, recognize their historical origins, accept their doctrinal and cultural differences, and go to heaven in their separate bodies, the Jews and Gentiles would have been saved in two different bodies. But God refused to accept that; both Jew and Gentile were reconciled to God in *one* body. There is no justification for modern denominationalism with its divisions.

Baptized Into One Body

How does one become a member of the Lord's body in which all men are reconciled to God? Paul answered that question with these words, "For by one Spirit are we all baptized into one body, whether we be Jews or Gentiles, whether we be bond or free; and have been all made to drink into one Spirit" (1 Cor. 12:13). Every man becomes a part of the body of Christ in the same way. There is one plan of salvation for every man, whether Jew or Gentile, male or female, rich or poor. In order to become a part of the body of Christ, a man must hear the gospel, believe it, repent of his sins, and be baptized into that one body. Those who have not done this are not members of the Lord's body, regardless of how well-intentioned they might be.

Jesus Is the Head of the Body

Paul emphasized the supreme authority of Christ, who is "far above all principality, and power, and might, and dominion, and every name that is named, not only in this world, but also in that which is come." He is "the head over all things to the church, which is his body" (Eph. 1:21-23). The comparison of Jesus to the head of the body also emphasizes the oneness of the church. A person has never seen one head attached to 1200 bodies, as would be necessary if Jesus were the head of every denomination. The comparison also emphasizes Jesus' position of authority over the church. The body does what its head directs.

Every body has only one head. Hence, Jesus is "head over all things to the church." A body with several different heads would be monstrous; yet, this is exactly what is demanded by modern denominationalism. Every denomination claims that Jesus is the head of the denomination. Yet, their members also claim that the pope or some synod or council is also governing head of the church. Legislative authority is granted to these earthly heads (papacy, synods, councils). Denominations conceive of their denominational body having more than one head. Which head is followed when there is conflict between the heads (Jesus versus the Pope, synod or council)?

Most denominations have an annual meeting during which laws are passed to govern the denomination. One group might meet to decide whether or not to ordain women and homosexuals as preachers; another might decide to condone or condemn abortion. Decisions are made by the body to govern the body. Not so with the body of Christ! The head directs and the body submits. What the head of the body, Jesus Christ, said about homosexuality governs the body; what the head said about the role of women regulates the body. The members of the church have no legislative role in the body; that is reserved for the head, Jesus Christ (Matt. 28:18).

By recognizing the authority of Jesus as head of the body, the members submit to Christ. Even as the members of my body respond to what the head directs, so also should members of the body of Christ respond to what the spiritual head, Jesus, directs. When my body parts act on their own (such as a twitching eyelid), they act without authority from the head, creating problems for the whole body. Similarly, when Christians act without divine authority, they create problems for the body of Christ.

Many Members Working Together

The comparison of the church to the body of Christ emphasizes the individual contribution that every member makes to the body of Christ (read 1 Cor. 12:14-21). The physical body needs what the eye, ear, foot, hand, heart, lung, etc. contribute. A body cannot exist and function properly without every member contributing what it can do. From this we learn these spiritual lessons:

1. Not every member can do the same job. We are not totally alike. Each of us can make a different contribution to the overall functioning of the body. We would err in trying to make every member contribute the same thing. We should not try to make a song leader out of every man, a teacher out of every person (1 Cor. 12:29), etc. Let every man see what he can contribute to the functioning of the body and assume his role.

> Having then gifts differing according to the grace that is given to us, whether prophecy, let us prophesy according to the proportion of faith; or ministry, let us wait on our ministering: or he that teacheth, on teaching; or he that exhorteth, on exhortation, he that giveth, let him do it with simplicity; he that ruleth, with diligence; he that sheweth mercy, with cheerfulness (Rom. 12:6-8).

> As every man hath received the gift, even so minister the same one to another, as good stewards of the manifold grace of God (1 Pet. 4:10).

2. The body depends upon the contribution of every part. "From whom the whole body fitly joined together and compacted by that which every joint supplieth, according to the effectual working in the measure of every part, maketh increase of the body unto the edifying of itself in love" (Eph. 4:16). A physical body with members that do not function is handicapped or retarded. The entire body is crippled by legs which cannot walk, eyes which do not see, and ears which cannot hear. Such a body cannot properly function. The same is true of the Lord's body, the church. A church full of non-functioning members is retarded in its work and handicapped. It can do very little or nothing. The church depends upon the contribution that every member can make to its overall work.

3. The members sometimes judged lesser important make the most important contribution. Paul said, "Nay, much more those members of the body, which seem to be more feeble, are necessary: and those members of the body, which we think to be less honorable, upon these we bestow more abundant honor" (1 Cor. 12:22-23). In the church at Corinth, the Christians esteemed the gift of tongue-speaking to be the most important contribution to the church and prophecy as less important. Paul wanted them to learn that prophecy was more important than tongue-speaking; hence, he emphasized that the less important members of the body are more necessary than those thought to be more important. Today, we sometimes esteem the more public servants of the church to be more important (preachers, those holding gospel meetings, etc.). We need to remember the importance of the contribution of every part of the body. I have seen churches exist without preachers and elders, but never without members!

4. *There should be no schism in the body.* "There should be no schism in the body," Paul emphasized (1 Cor. 12:25). There should exist no rivalry between the members of the body of Christ. In my physical body, the left hand is not in competition with the right foot. Rather, they work together for the body to function properly. Similarly, there should be no rivalry among the members of the church. They work together for the overall good of the whole body.

5. *The members should have the same care one for another.* To emphasize this care, Paul added, "And whether one member suffer, all the members suffer with it; or one member be honoured, all the members rejoice with it" (1 Cor. 12:26). The intimacy of the members is emphasized by the figure of the body. As Christians, we should learn to care for one another, sharing each others joys and sorrows.

Conclusion

Are you a member of the body of Christ? A Christian is a member of the body of Christ. Many who profess to be Christians are members of some other body, never having done what is necessary to become a member of the body of Christ (1 Cor. 12:13). Others who profess to be Christians make no contribution to the overall functioning of the body. Are they really Christians?

Questions

1. How many bodies did Christ have in the first century (Eph. 4:4)? _____
   How many does he have in this century? _____
2. Where does reconciliation to God occur (Eph. 2:16)? _____
   _____
3. Did God approve of one body for the Jews and another body for the Gentiles (Eph. 2:16)? _____
   Will he approve of one body for Baptists, another for Methodists, another for Catholics, etc. today? _____
4. If Jesus is the Savior of the body (Eph. 5:23), how many outside the body

will be saved? _____

5. How does one become a member of the body (1 Cor. 12:13)? _____
_____

6. What part of the body is Jesus (Eph. 1:22)? _____

7. Of how many bodies is he the head? _____

8. What is emphasized by the figure of Jesus being the head of the body?
_____

9. What right does the church have to make laws (Matt. 28:18; Jas. 4:12)?
_____

10. Why should we not require every member to teach, preach, lead singing,
etc. (1 Cor. 12:14-21)? _____
_____

11. Since the body functions through that which every member supplies,
what do you supply for the functioning of this church (1 Cor. 12:14-21)?
_____
_____

12. If the whole church functioned just like me, the church would . . . _____
_____

13. Which members of the spiritual body are the most important? _____
_____

14. Why should there be no schism in the body (1 Cor. 12:25)? _____
_____

15. What impact does division have on the body? _____
_____

16. What must happen in order for members to suffer and rejoice with one
another (1 Cor. 12:26)? _____
_____

17. Do Christians sin by telling others the causes of their sorrows? _____
_____

18. What keeps sharing joys and sorrows from occurring? _____
_____

19. What can we do to contribute toward greater intimacy in this local congregation? _____
_____

A Christian . . . Wears A Worthy Name

When James wrote to condemn showing respect of persons toward the rich, he said, "Do not they (the rich, mw) blaspheme that *worthy name* by the which ye are called?" (2:7) The name by which the Lord's people are called is "Christian." The word appears only these three times in the New Testament:

... And the disciples were called Christians first in Antioch (Acts 11:26).

Then Agrippa said unto Paul, Almost thou persuadest me to be a Christian (Acts 26:28).

Yet if any man suffer as a Christian, let him not be ashamed; but let him glorify God on this behalf (1 Pet. 4:16).

Those who are followers of Christ are designated Christians. They wear the name of Christ. 1 Corinthians 1:10-13 emphasizes that one should wear the name of him who died for us and in whose name we were baptized. The wearing of other names, such as Baptist, Methodist, Episcopalian, Presbyterian, Catholic, etc., is condemned by these verses.

The Name Is Divinely Given

In Acts 11:26, Luke records, "And the disciples were called Christians first in Antioch." That the name Christian was divinely given and it is subsequently used to describe the followers of Christ made this a notable occasion. The record states that at Antioch the gospel message was preached to Gentiles (11:20). The news of the conversion of the Gentiles caused the apostles at Jerusalem to send Barnabas to see what was happening there. When he arrived in Antioch, he saw the grace of God. He went to Antioch and brought Saul of Tarsus to work with him there. For a whole year, they taught much people. Paul and Barnabas called the disciples Christians first at Antioch.[1]

---

[1] The construction of the language seems to imply that "they" (meaning Barnabas and Saul) "called" the disciples Christians. "They" is obviously the subject of the verbs "assembled" and "taught." The subject of the verb "were called" (an active verb, not passive as is usually translated) is implied, not stated. The most logical subject is "they." Hence, under divine inspiration, Paul and Barnabas called the disciples Christians first at Antioch (F. J. Foakes Jackson and Kirsopp Lake [*The Beginnings of*

The giving of the name was under divine inspiration.[2]

On this occasion, for the first time, both Jews and Gentiles were brought into the body of Christ on equal footing.

> It was a new era – a grand epoch, which would have an important bearing on its future progress to the end of time. It was the first decided step in the creation of one new man, composed of Jews and Gentiles; and of breaking down the middle wall of partition between them. It was the reconciling both unto God in one body by the cross, having slain the enmity in himself. The far off and the nigh, were now brought together into one loving fraternity. The Gentiles were no longer strangers and foreigners, but fellow-citizens with the saints, and of the household of God. It was fitting that this new family, new community – *new man*, should have a *new* name.[3]

The Lord acknowledged this significant event by giving the disciples a new name – the name Christian.[4] The term "Christian" distinguishes God's people from all others; it points to believers as the property of Christ; it includes all who are his disciples (there is no room for "kinds" of Christians, such as Baptist Christian, Methodist Christian, etc.).

The Meaning of the Name

The name "Christian" is formed from the word "Christ" and the Latinized ending -*ianos*. The word is defined to mean "a follower of Christ." The word "Christ" (anointed), in contrast to the personal name of Jesus, points to the Messianic promises being fulfilled in Jesus of Nazareth. One who wears the name "Christian" identifies himself as a believer in the work of God through the Messiah. He acknowledges his faith in the promises to Abraham, Isaac, Jacob, David, etc. being fulfilled in Jesus of Nazareth, the son of Mary. He confesses his dependency upon the atoning blood of Jesus for salvation.

Too, he confesses his commitment to walk in the footsteps of Jesus. "Thus

---

Christianity, Vol. III, p. 130] acknowledge that if *chrematizo* is active, Saul and Barnabas is the subject of the verb). If Saul and Barnabas did not give the name, its origin is lost. The Jews obviously did not give the name to the disciples (because of their own concepts of the Messiah). Most commentaries state that the name was given to the disciples by the Gentiles as a term of derision, though no evidence is produced to support the idea. A more logical and grammatical explanation is that Saul and Barnabas gave the name under divine inspiration.

[2] The verb "were called" is translated from *chrematizo* which occurs nine times in the Scriptures. The word means "to be divinely commanded, admonished, instructed." Hence, the calling was a divine calling.

[3] *Lard's Quarterly*, Vol. I, pp. 386-387.

[4] Some see additional evidence of the divine origin of the name "Christian" in these prophecies from Isaiah: 56:5; 62:1-4; 65:15. While I am unconvinced that these passages foretell the giving of the name Christian, I am convinced that the name Christian is divinely given.

they were called Christians because they were like Christ. They had his spirit. They possessed his benevolence. They had fairly won the pre-eminent distinction of being called by his name. . . . But having received the name, are we worthy of wearing it? Have we the singleness of heart and purpose; the spirit and temper; the benevolence and missionary enterprise; have we the likeness of Christ, which characterized the disciples at Antioch?"[5]

Are You A Christian?

Are you a follower of Christ? Have you imbibed his spirit and committed yourself to walking in his footsteps? Here are a few areas of application:

1. His spirit of obedience. Jesus came to do the will of the Father (Jn. 5:30; 8:28-29). He submitted to the Father's will even when his own desires were in conflict with the Father's will (Matt. 26:39). Many of us are quite willing to obey the Father so long as our will agrees with his commandments. But, when what God wants us to do conflicts with our own will, some refuse to obey.

2. His spirit toward his personal enemies. Jesus taught men to pray for their enemies (Matt. 5:38-48) and to forgive those who sin against us (Matt. 18:21-35). One never sees a hateful, vindictive spirit in Christ. While on the cross he left an example of how to act toward one's enemies. Despite his sufferings at the hands of those who mocked, physically abused, and crucified him, Jesus prayed for the Lord to forgive them (Lk. 23:34). His example in suffering is worthy to follow (1 Pet. 2:21-25). He was like a lamb dumb before the shearer, with reference to personal offence.

3. His spirit of love. Jesus manifested his great love for mankind in laying down his life in order that men might be saved from sin (Jn. 10:17-18; Rom. 5:6-9). His work in teaching the gospel was to seek and save that which was lost (Lk. 19:10). Without any selfish motivation, Jesus suffered willingly that others may be saved. Many practice good-will for selfish reasons; Jesus gained nothing from his self-sacrificing love for us.

4. His attitude toward false teachers. Whereas Jesus might be compared to a lamb, with reference to how he suffered personal abuse without retaliation, he was the lion out of the tribe of Judah (Rev. 5:5) with reference to his conduct toward false teachers (Matt. 23:1-33; 15:1 9, 13-14; 21:12-13). He manifested an unyielding spirit toward the doctrine of Christ; he was unwilling to give up one truth of God's word for the sake of unity. Many have been unwilling to manifest this spirit of Christ; they have become more "loving" than Christ toward false teachers. They say, "Don't knock other religions," "Don't call names from the pulpit," "Preachers are too negative," etc. to undermine exposing the false religions of our age. That they do this in the

---

[5] *Ibid.*, pp. 390-391.

name of the "sweet spirit" of Christ, when Christ never manifested this spirit toward false teaching, is ironic.

5. His moral purity and spiritual mindedness. Jesus was tempted in all points like as we are, but did not yield to sin (Heb. 4:15). He left us a perfect example of how to walk in the pathway of righteousness. He was totally committed to the obedience to God, not being distracted by the cares of this world to the extent that God was rooted out of his life or given a second place. He abstained from drunkenness, fornication, homosexuality, theft, lying, extortion, embezzling, etc. He showed love, joy, peace, longsuffering, patience, kindness, etc. in his life.

6. His evangelistic zeal. Jesus said, "For the son of man is come to seek and to save that which was lost" (Lk. 19:10). His life was totally devoted to accomplishing this goal. He worked hard saying, "I must work the works of him that sent me, while it is day: the night cometh, when no man can work" (Jn. 9:4). He gave the parable of the lost sheep in which the shepherd left the 99 in search of the one sheep that was lost (Lk. 15:1-7). This was how he lived. He sought the one lost sheep in the woman at the well (Jn. 4), the woman taken in the act of adultery (Jn. 8:1-11), the woman with a bad reputation who anointed him with oil and washed his feet with her tears (Lk. 7:38-44), and in Zaccheus, the publican who was rejected by his society (Lk. 19:1-10). He then charged his disciples to go into all the world and preach his gospel to every creature (Mk. 16:15-16).

Conclusion

Are you a Christian? Many who wear the name obviously aren't Christians. But what about you? Are you the child of God, believer, saint, soldier, worker, etc. that you should be? A Christian is. Let us glorify the name of God by our conduct.

Questions

1. List the three passages in which the word "Christian" appears. _____
   _____

2. What two requirements must be met before one wears another's name, according to 1 Corinthians 1:10-13? _____
   _____

3. How does 1 Corinthians 1:10-13 forbid the wearing of such names as Baptist, Methodist, Episcopalian, Catholics, etc.? _____
   _____
   _____

4. How did the disciples get the name Christian? _____
   _____

5. What does "Christian" mean? _____

6. What spirit of obedience did Christ manifest (Jn. 5:30; 8:28-29)? _____

7. When there was a conflict between what he desired to do and what God required of him, what did Jesus do (Matt. 26:39)? _____

8. What spirit did Jesus teach that one should show toward his enemies (Matt. 5:38-48)? _____

9. What spirit did he manifest toward those who crucified him (Lk. 23:34; 1 Pet. 2:21-25)? _____

10. Describe Jesus' spirit of love toward mankind (Jn. 10:17-18; Rom. 5:6-9)? _____

11. Why did his spirit of love allow him to rebuke sinners? _____

12. What spirit did Jesus manifest toward false teachers (Matt. 23:1-33; 15:1-9)? _____

13. Why was he so hard on them? _____

14. What spirit did Jesus show toward the works of the flesh? _____

15. Did he want to see just how close to sin he could come without actually touching it? _____

16. How would you describe Jesus' attitude toward saving the lost (Lk. 15:1-7)? _____

17. Can a person be a Christian without manifesting the spirit of Christ? ___

www.ingramcontent.com/pod-product-compliance
Lightning Source LLC
Chambersburg PA
CBHW021139020426
42331CB00005B/838